New Approaches
to Medieval Textuality

Studies on Themes and Motifs in Literature

Horst S. Daemmrich
General Editor

Vol. 28

PETER LANG
New York • Washington, D.C./Baltimore • Boston
Bern • Frankfurt am Main • Berlin • Vienna • Paris

New Approaches
to Medieval Textuality

Edited by
Mikle Dave Ledgerwood

PETER LANG
New York • Washington, D.C./Baltimore • Boston
Bern • Frankfurt am Main • Berlin • Vienna • Paris

Library of Congress Cataloging-in-Publication Data

New approaches to medieval textuality / Mikle Dave Ledgerwood, editor.
p. cm. — (Studies on themes and motifs in literature; vol. 28)
Includes bibliographical references.
1. English literature—Middle English, 1100–1500—Criticism, Textual.
2. English poetry—Old English, ca. 450–1100—Criticism, Textual.
3. Mysteries and miracle plays, English—Criticism, Textual. 4. Literature,
Medieval—Criticism, Textual. 5. Ballads, English—Criticism, Textual.
6. Manuscripts, Medieval—Editing. 7. Oral tradition—Great Britain.
8. Semiotics and literature. I. Ledgerwood, Mikle Dave. II. Series.
PR275.T45N47   820.9'001—dc20   95-40414
ISBN 0-8204-3026-9
ISSN 1056-3970

Die Deutsche Bibliothek-CIP-Einheitsaufnahme

New approaches to medieval textuality / Mikle Dave Ledgerwood, ed.
—New York; Washington, D.C./Baltimore; Boston; Bern;
Frankfurt am Main; Berlin; Vienna; Paris: Lang.
(Studies on themes and motifs in literature; Vol. 28)
ISBN 0-8204-3026-9
NE: Ledgerwood, Mikle Dave. [Hrsg.]; GT

The paper in this book meets the guidelines for permanence and durability
of the Committee on Production Guidelines for Book Longevity
of the Council of Library Resources.

Printed in the United States of America.

CONTENTS

PREFACE

Medieval literary studies have been at a crossroads for some years now. While discussions of hypertext, multi-culturalism, CD-Rom, and political correctness become more and more normative, a good part of medieval studies seems still bound to modes of formalist criticism and questions like which text is the most authoritative. Even the electronic mail network of Anglo-Saxonists has spent hours in trying to answer the question of whether the hero of the Anglo-Saxon epic should be called Beowulf or Beowa. There are other questions to pursue. Indeed, issues and arguments that have excited many other late twentieth-century literary scholars also pertain to medieval literature.

Jonathan Evans of the University of Georgia decided to test this hypothesis. As a medieval scholar very interested in new theoretical perspectives, he began to work on identifying other medievalists with similar interests and soon collected a list of fifty scholars. He asked these scholars to produce work using various theoretical approaches for sessions at different academic meetings. While he noted how exciting these papers were, he also noticed that many of the them were not being published. As a result, he decided to edit a special volume of *Semiotica* to be published in conjunction with *Style*. In 1987, he decided to go one step farther and contacted all the scholars he knew who had an interest in the fields of semiotics and medieval textuality. He asked them to participate in a colloquium on this topic with the hope of exploring medieval textuality fully. Twelve scholars responded by presenting papers over three days and discussing the issues raised in a final plenary session on the last day of the meeting. They realized that the colloquium's result was a distinct contribution to medieval textuality.

A group of scholars previously unknown to each other from different academic disciplines in different countries had come together. Using the language of semiotics they had expressed through their own subfields their thoughts on how to approach questions of medieval textuality from their various theoretical perspectives. It became clear that a group of these papers should be assembled and published so that others with an interest in medieval literature and in questions of text/textuality could benefit from their work. It was 1989 before all the papers were collected. George Wingerter of Austin College and myself undertook the task to edit them, and by early 1990, we selected the final articles and began the process of editing them.

Then, unfortunately, in September 1990, George Wingerter died of an embolism while walking across campus. We dedicate this book to him—to a scholar who reminded those who knew him that students learn best from laughter.

I remain to thank all the contributors to this volume, especially George Wingerter, Jonathan Evans, and Sun Hee Geertz who did the final reading of the text. I am also extremely grateful for the generous assistance given me by Marjorie Stoner while I was at Rhodes College and to Kris Vandenberg here at Stony Brook. Finally, I wish to thank my family for giving me the time and support necessary to finish this project, and I am especially grateful to my wife, Fayanne Thorngate.

Mikle D. Ledgerwood
University at Stony Brook
Stony Brook, New York

INTRODUCTION

This collection gives a variety of scholars a chance to address the issue of medieval textuality from varying theoretical perspectives. The book contains seven chapters, each representing different areas of exploration, study, or critical focus. Taken as a whole, they point to new directions for medieval studies.

In three of the chapters—the first, the third, and the fifth—theoretical interests predominate, with the first invoking the Kuhnian paradigm, the third, a specifically oral *Rezeptionstheorie*, and the fifth, Lacanian psychology. In the remaining chapters, attention is focused on the more narrow study of texts and textuality in essays that demonstrate the richness and complexity of the world of medieval Europe.

The first essay in the book by Jonathan Evans contains two parts. The first and longer part outlines the problems medieval criticism has had with many twentieth-century theoretical notions. Not just semiotics (both in its European and its American forms), but also the new hermeneutics, phenomenology, and ethnic or gender theory have been ignored by medieval scholars until recently. Evans explores the reasons for this attitude and proposes a new paradigm for medieval studies. In the second part of his essay, he then gives an example of the type of direction he proposes by looking at how pictorial images contained in manuscripts can be read as texts. His final purpose is to discuss and propose eliminating the positivistic and pseudo-scientific *stemmata* theory of manuscripts.

The next two chapters take up the problem of texts which were originally orally transmitted. The second essay thus studies the medieval ballad, specifically that of the British Isles. Karin Boglund-Lagopoulos examines how we can classify ballads and discuss their textuality in the context of more traditionally-studied works. Using the Greimassian terms of isotopy and code, she isolates new groupings of ballads. In the third chapter, Mikle Ledgerwood examines ballads as well as other orally produced texts, focusing on early French and Welsh. He discusses how their structure is not an incomplete series of often redundant episodes, but narratives produced with the intention of allowing the listener to participate in them. He then projects his conclusions towards other oral texts.

The next two essays, chapters four and five, address specific problems of medieval drama. The first of these, by SunHee Kim Gertz, discusses how language and staging can extend a play's meaning through theatrical modification of conventionally accepted signs, using the Digby *Mary Magdalene* as her example. In chapter five, Mavis Fionella examines the Towneley passion plays from the perspective of Lacanian theory to suggest what potential role they can play in an understanding of Christian subjectivity, especially the type of subjectivity experienced by the play's audience.

The sixth chapter, by Lois Bragg, moves into yet another area of textuality, Old English metrical charms. In her essay, she analyzes many different charms, which she defines as everything associated with a spell, both the magical incantation as well as the directions on how to accomplish the spell. She thereby probes the relationship between the magical and the literary, or the performative and the aesthetic components of a spell.

The last chapter in the book, by Gary Shank, treats various medieval bestiaries. In his analysis, he employs many different terms from the world of computers to explain how the medieval bestiary is essentially an Expert Systems Database (ESD) with its own operating system (OS). To be sure, the bestiaries must be understood in terms of their own time, yet posing their function as an ESD also allows us to comprehend the interest modern creative writers still have in this genre.

As a group these essays show how varied medieval textual criticism can be. Ranging from dragon drawings to oral performances and databases, this collection demonstrates the versatility medieval textuality and medieval theory can take.

Mikle D. Ledgerwood
University at Stony Brook
Stony Brook, New York

CHAPTER ONE

A CONSIDERATION OF THE ROLE OF SEMIOTICS IN REDEFINING MEDIEVAL MANUSCRIPTS AS TEXTS

Jonathan Evans

PART ONE: SEMIOTICIZATION OF MEDIEVAL STUDIES

If we could be certain that the history of science and the history of critical theory in the humanities were analogous, it would be easy to suggest that current developments in medieval studies seem to point toward a radical shift of such implications as to indicate a fundamental redefinition of the basic paradigms upon which medieval studies has traditionally based its activity. While these developments may represent nothing more than the desire of a growing number of medievalists educated in the philological and New Critical tradition to draw into their own work some of the perspectives fostered by recent developments in literary/critical/theoretical circles, there is reason enough to believe that they represent something larger. Indulging the semiotician's penchant for the use of polysyllabic neologisms—which admittedly serves the purpose of mystification partly for the sake of social identification by exclusion—we might characterize this process as the "semioticization" of medieval studies and as a wholesale shift in our understanding of medieval textuality. In the last decade, time-honored presuppositions about the principal tasks of medieval scholarship and dogmatic conceptions about the nature of medieval literature have become subject to revision, redefinition, revamping and—sometimes—discarding. Current developments of this kind represent the effect of some seventy years of research in the nature of textuality, particularly the last quarter-century of semiotic scholarship, that have so altered the underlying conception of textuality as to have an impact not only upon the disciplines closest to the avant-garde—e.g., modern and post-modern literature and literary criticism; film theory; French studies; popular culture—but also upon the rear-guard of Western culture in medieval studies.

The present crisis: pre-paradigm?

If this is an accurate description, we must admit immediately that we are at present unable to detail with certainty all the features of the new paradigm, whose very emergence can only be a matter of conjecture. Even to suggest that we are somewhere in what Thomas S. Kuhn called the "pre-paradigm" stage may prejudice the question in advance with a degree of surety which may be unwarranted. Some similarities between the present state of medieval studies and Kuhn's description of this stage seem evident, and it may be worthwhile here to consider for a moment the development of this concept in Kuhn's thought in order to identify its usefulness in describing the current state of affairs in medieval studies.

"The pre-paradigm stage," Kuhn wrote,

> ...is regularly marked by frequent and deep debates over legitimate methods, problems, and standards of solution, though these serve rather to define schools than to produce agreement. (Kuhn 47–48)

Kuhn's thoughts on the subject of paradigms appears to have evolved over a period of years partly in response to the reception of his essential thesis, which was published in 1962. In the second edition of his *Structure of Scientific Revolutions* (1970), in a "Postscript" to this original thesis, Kuhn expands and refines his original definition of "paradigm" to include the following elements: the shared commitments of a scientific community, objectified in a "disciplinary matrix" consisting of "symbolic generalizations" and metaphorical components including "beliefs," on a "spectrum from heuristic to ontological models," "preferred or permissible analogies and metaphors," "values" and "exemplars"—all of this amounting to tacit knowledge which the novice acquires "through training as a part of his preparation for group-membership." Kuhn suggests there that the communal/ social component of the process of scientific discovery is paramount, with implications that we can see as *rhetorical* rather than epistemological: when the shared commitments and tacit knowledge breaks down, he suggests, a lack of communication between researchers develops which is bridged primarily through *persuasion* and through *translation* from one group to another.

Kuhn's description of the pre-paradigm stage later, in a 1974 essay entitled "Second Thoughts on Paradigms" reveals a still further refinement on the description of this stage given earlier: during what is called, in *Structure of Scientific Revolutions*, the "pre-paradigm period," the practioners of a science are split into a number of competing schools, each claiming competence for the same subject matter but approaching it in quite different ways [Kuhn (b) 295]. This stage is followed by a transition period, usually after a significant scientific breakthrough, to a "post-paradigm period characterized by the disappearance of all or most schools..." The pattern is "typical and important," and paradigms "are possessed by any scientific community, including the schools of the so-called pre-paradigm period." His failure to see this clearly helped to make the concept of paradigm "seem a quasi-mystical entity or property which, like charisma, transforms those infected by it. There is a transformation, but it is not induced by the acquisition of a paradigm" (ibid). In other words, we may deduce, the pre-paradigm state is one characterized by rivalry between schools, each with its own set of prescribed standards of inquiry, tools, methods of investigation, and projections of anticipated solutions. The acceptance of a paradigm at the level of the whole discipline involves the triumph of one school and its paradigm over all the others, with a consequent disappearance of the awareness of the paradigm implicit in the discipline and the history that has brought about the change. Kuhn's 1962 discussion of the role of textbooks in the retrospective rewriting of scientific history is most illuminating and should cause medievalists to pause for serious reflection on the implications of this line of thinking for their own discipline.

Evidence supporting the notion that medieval studies has reached a state of crisis may be gathered from a variety of sources, including scholarly articles. Although whole issues of journals have been dedicated to theoretical questions in medieval studies, yet—perhaps more significantly—conference papers interrogating fundamental medieval-studies issues for a variety of reasons, including conscious suppression by more traditionally-minded editors, fail to see the light of publication. (I have not assembled statistical evidence in support of this point, but even an unsystematic survey of conference programs of the MLA and its regional affiliates and of the annual congress of the Medieval Institute in Kalamazoo reveals a growing recognition of the need to reevaluate the fundamental theories underlying most of what has been taken for granted in medieval scholarship. No one who has attended such conferences and participated in the conversations can fail to acknowledge this. Further, when the evident interest in these matters is compared to current publications in the field, it is obvious that a greater proportion of theoretically-oriented papers have been read in recent years than have been published. Of course such a disproportion generally occurs in any discipline, but it could be said that in medieval studies the normal winnowing process works with peculiar convenience to prevent papers that confront the most basic questions—and, arguably the most important ones—from being published.)

The defining features of the pre-paradigm stage in the history of science lead to the suspicion that we may be in the middle of a transition period in medieval studies. By definition, it is impossible to judge the veracity of this surmise until after the putative shift is fully complete—and by that time, many of the scholars currently involved in this stage in the history of medieval studies (including the present volume's readers) will be gone. It may be best to proceed, then, under an assumption, tempered by *humilitas*, that if present trends continue, the current movement in medieval studies towards a greater awareness of the theoretical issues underlying the discipline may lead to further exploration down a path to redefinition. Indeed, the proper attitude of scientific inquiry is perhaps best described by the injunction "wait and doubt."

In 1979, Hans Robert Jauss accounted for this state of affairs in this way:

> The present dilemma of research into the Middle Ages may be sketched as follows: the classical paradigms of the positivistic research of tradition as well as of the idealistic interpretation of works or styles have exhausted themselves, and the highly touted modern methods of structural linguistics, semiotics, and phenomenological or sociological literary theory have not yet gelled into the development of paradigms. [Jauss (a) 182]

Jauss proposed a hermeneutic method in response to this situation that embraces the surprising and pleasurable "alterity" or otherness of the medieval text as a way of overcoming the gaps

between modern response and the horizon of expectation which
defined the context of meaning for the medieval audience for
which it was originally intended. By seeking to fuse our modern
expectations concerning the æsthetic experience with the
expectations of the medieval audience (so far as we are able to
determine them), says Jauss, we can save medieval research from
simple antiquarianism and rescue the teaching of medieval texts
from curricular obscurity [Jauss (a) 182–184].   The fusing of
modern with medieval expectation thus complicated the tasks
involved in the modern analysis, exegesis, and critique of medieval
materials. Yet semiotics may be uniquely suited to this complex of
related activities.

Tasks

If a new paradigm is emergent in medieval studies, and if
semiotics indeed promises to contribute to its definition, then
medieval semiotic studies has a threefold obligation: (1) to search
for explicit theories of the sign and signification in medieval
learning itself; (2) to extricate implied or embedded theories of the
sign from medieval cultural materials; and (3) to apply modern
semiotic theory to the analysis and criticism of cultural artifacts
from the Middle Ages (see Evans).   The operations of this
enterprise reveal a number of differences between medieval and
modern conceptions of textuality, particularly in narratives, that
grew out of 19th-century romanticism into the dominant genres of
textuality in the Victorian and early modern period, e.g., of
English literary history and helped to form the most successful
body of English-language criticism in this century: New Criticism.
It has been suggested that in fact medieval literary theory itself
has far greater affinities with postmodern developments in theory
and criticism than with the New Critical school:

> ...there is much in medieval literary theory and criticism which
> seems contrary to the spirit of at least one of 'the major schools
> of criticism characteristic of our age, namely 'New Criticism').
> John Dryden, who has a certain claim to be regarded as the
> founding father of that movement, speaks of criticisms as 'a
> standard of judging well; the chiefest part of which is, to
> observe those excellences which should delight a reasonable
> reader" This emphasis on delighting a reasonable reader, with
> its overtones of the good taste and humanistic virtue of a group
> of initiates, is quite at variance with the priorities of medieval

literary theory, which is concerned with profit rather than with delight as such and assumes that reason is a God-given faculty which should operate to bring the individual into line with the great divine plan. Hence, all that is written is, in the final analysis, written for our doctrine (to echo Rom. 15:4); more specifically, to make us better Christians. Seen in this light, medieval literary theory and criticism has far more in common with the ideologically-based and philosophically-patterned types of 'New New Criticism' which are currently in vogue; in particular, with formalism, structuralism, semiotics, and reception-theory, and especially with those approaches which have a sharply defined teleology, such as feminist criticism, and political criticism of whatever persuasion. Of more fundamental importance is the fact that nowadays it is being claimed, *pace* the 'Old New Critics', that *no* criticism is free of ideology, that every approach to a text reflects, and is ultimately dependent on, a particular world-view. (Minnis & Scott: viii–ix)

Hence the fourth and most important role of semiotics in the disciplinary revolution in which we may now be engaged: the critique of the discipline itself and its underlying assumptions (see Evans). The assumptions that seem to inform the discipline could be described as a sort of "sacred secularist" preoccupation with the editorial establishment, pedagogical transmission, and hermeneutic exegesis of texts whose cultural function serves a quest for the origin of and justification for Western culture. In this connection it is not irrelevant to point out that the rise of medieval studies in this century corresponds with the accelerated expansion of the universities in American society especially in the period following the second World War with the appearance and development of New Criticism in the undergraduate classroom. This development may be likened to the rise of the secular universities in the twelfth century, since it represents the secularization of a system of American college education founded upon, and in service to, a religious, specifically Christian world-view. Whereas the older system of American colleges, like the ecclesiastical and monastic schools of the earlier middle ages, served the Church to a greater or lesser extent with their ultimate goals being the transmission and elucidation of Scripture, so the newer secularized system of university education found its goals in the transmission and elucidation of its own (culturally) sacred texts. The Church has its exegetical tradition, and so has the university: the New Critical conception of the text as verbal icon and the priestly role of the university professor as mediator of the text's hermetic meaning may be more than accidentally related to the goal and functions of the medieval university's textual preoccupations (particularly in the *trivium*) identified first with the Hebrew and Christian Scriptures and later—beginning with the twelfth-century renaissance—with the poetic and historical texts of European culture.

Defining medieval textuality: overcoding the intertext

The fruits of interchange between medieval studies and the theories of textuality promulgated in semiotic studies reveal a number of textual features divergent from modern expectations; a number of these have been discussed in print, three of which seem to me to be salient: (1) the highly *intertextual* character of medieval textuality; (2) the narratological dependence upon microstructural regulation rather than macrostructural (e.g., "plot-level") unity: i.e., *episodic* structure; and (3) the highly-developed degree to which medieval textuality seems to have been subject to *overcoding*. The first and the third of these three occupy the focus of this essay.

The term "overcoding" and the concept it defines are somewhat unfamiliar to readers brought up in a more traditional paradigm, and so some elaboration here seems warranted. Umberto Eco develops this concept in the context of a theory of codes that is at the heart of his *Theory of Semiotics,* and which is too complex to summarize here. For Eco, however, the expression of meaning in semiosis is the result of correlating units of meaning with units of expression according to sets of rules governing this process of correlation. This is how language operates, and it is how literary texts use language in order to induce the perception of story, character, setting, theme, and so on. Now *overcoding*, according to this theory, is defined in this way: "on the basis of a pre-established rule, a new rule was proposed which governed a rarer application of the previous rule" [Eco (a): 133].

Overcoding applies rules of a second order to those of a first. To give an example, coding of the first level is what happens when we correlate the idea of a rose with the phonetic structure we hear when, in English, we pronounce the word "rose." Coding of the second level, or overcoding, occurs when we correlate the previous coded entity, the /rose/sign, with the idea of romantic love.

Presumably, this correlation has a biological element: the color red represents passion by association with the flushing of cheeks and the engorgement of lips, etc., with sexual arousal. The mutually-entailed correlations might be drawn thus:

/Rose/ = /red/ = /blood/ = /passion/ = /love/

Since Saussure, however, we have known that in both cases there is nothing motivating such correlations except convention—linguistic, in first-order coding; cultural in the second—as we can imagine a literary tradition in which the association between the color red and the color of blood would cause red roses to signify violence and bloodshed and hence death; here we can see, by the way, one possible explanation of the relationship between the literary themes of love and death, both of them originating in blood, with a genealogy on one side of the tree generating a pedigree based upon passion and the other side (generating relations based on violence. In the instance of first-order coding, the relationship between the idea and the name of the rose is arbitrary and conventional (but legitimized by literary tradition); in the instance of overcoding it is doubly conventional, since the secondary meaning of the rose depends crucially upon the first if it is to have any meaning. And of course still another level of overcoding underlies the present paragraph, correlating as it does the name of Eco and the name of the rose, whose usage as the title of a novel and the movie based upon it looms large in the margins of the present discourse.

These trivial examples suggest something of what goes on in linguistic utterances that depart from their simple denotata to convey information connotatively, of which the example most generally interesting to us is the literary text. And it further suggests how literary language can be an important vehicle which, especially in the case of cultural alterity, helps us understand a culture's peculiar attempt to come to grips with its experiences at a particular place in a particular period of time.

As Eco points out, if the establishment of a new rule governing a "rarer application of the previous rule" becomes completely accepted by a social group, then the result is a *subcode*. "[I]n this sense," says Eco, "overcoding is an innovatory activity that increasingly loses its provocative power, thereby producing social acceptance." Thus what starts out as creation, innovation, invention, etc., ends up as just another code, another convention, another ossified instance of predictability standing ready for the next overcoding procedure to produce yet another subcode which in turn will go on to become a conventional code in its own right. We can imagine, then, our correlation between red roses and violent death, as originating first as a violation of the dominant æsthetic code, then as an instance of ironic overcoding, emerging finally in literary tradition as the dominant code.

This is not likely to occur, however, because as Eco goes on to say, "more frequently the overcoded entities float—so to speak—among the codes, on the threshold between convention and innovation. It is by a slow and prudent process that a society admits them to the ranks of the rules upon which it bases its very *raison d'être*. Frequently a society does not recognize overcoded rules that in fact allow the social exchange of sign." It is this indeterminacy of meaning that makes the semiotic analysis of any social or cultural group so fascinating, and which makes the analysis of cultural artifacts, including texts, from a bygone era so complex and potentially so fruitful: we can often come face to face with cultural meanings that would never have been articulated as such by the inhabitants of a culture but which nevertheless explain social behavior which otherwise would appear to be without context.

The "typical example" that Eco gives of overcoding is well suited to my purpose in this paper: the rules of narrative developed by Vladimir Propp in the *Morphology of the Folktale*, a proposal that "brought to light the existence of an overcoded language"—the laws of a narrative subcode which Eco says "are now universally accepted" and must lie deep at the heart of Western understanding of what makes a well-formed narrative, one whose relations with other narratives are perceived implicitly to be normative.

Overcoding and intertextuality are two mutually-related concepts, a connection that has been made by Eco: "This principle [of intertextuality] seems to me to join the one of overcoding, because only by means of overcoding is one able to refer an actual text to a series of previous texts in which something similar 'happened'... ." Quoting Eliseo Veron, Eco goes on to suggest that

L'analyse de ces textes et de ces codes qui n'apparaissent pas à la surface d'un discours donné mais qui cependant ont fait partie du processus de production de ce dernier, me semble essentielle: leur étude peut nous offrir des eclaircissements

> fondamentaux sur le processus de production lui-même et aussi sur la lecture du discours au niveau de la réception ... Ces discours 'cachés' (l'on peut songer aussi, par exemple, aux croquis et dessins des projets d'architecture) jouent un rôle instrumental dans la production d'un certain objet discursif et par la même constituent un lieu privilegié où transparaissent certains des mécanismes idéologiques à l'œuvre dans la production. Ils relèvent, si l'on peut dire, d'une intertextualité 'en profondeur', puisque ce sont des textes qui, faisant partie du processus de production d'autres textes, n'arrivent jamais eux-mêmes (ou très rarement, ou par des canaux très restreints) à la consommation sociale des discours.[1]

Linguistic utterances tend to borrow from prior utterances to add levels of meaning; this occurs at all levels of language-use, including both the oral and the written. In the middle ages, the written word was particularly prone to the incorporation of utterances previously composed and previously inscribed; manuscripts of texts therefore represent patchworks, forcing us to replace our modern works-immanent conception of the literary text with that of a plurality of texts of textual voices each speaking from its own rhetorical vantage-point to the central social concerns of the culture they inhabit, express, define, interrogate and critique. We emerge with a conception of narrative as a cultural space, a form, in which these rival voices compete for dominance in the incessant rhetorical labor that is involved in the attempt to answer the fundamental questions concerning human life, destiny, justice, joy, truth, and so on—a narrative whose major themes are at the bottom of any culture's preoccupations, whether this be an activity regarded as work or rather as play, as an activity that belongs properly to the sphere of the rational and (ultimately) the theological, or, on the other hand, to that of the irrational and ludic and (ultimately) the absurd.

It is for this reason that in the study of medieval literature in particular, whose multivariate labyrinth of manuscripts stands in such stark contrast to the monism of our modern concept of the authoritative printed edition, we must be ready to accord value to the so-called "valueless" manuscripts that by whatever process of censure have often failed to be taken seriously into account in the study of medieval culture. In the case of Old Icelandic sagas, from which my main examples will be drawn and where the rubber meets the road in the *application* of these ideas to actual textual material, Foster W. Blaisdell argued precisely in favor of a more careful look at manuscripts that an earlier generation of textual editors denominated as worthless, often in simple ignorance of the problems they can solve in the establishment of a definitive edition. In fact, we may go a step further, seeing the goal of medieval textual scholarship not only in the effort to establish "the" text of "the work" but also the reverse: to come to the point of seeing every manuscript, however corrupt, fragmentary, or derivative, as an individual voice in the global social dialogue of medieval culture.

The reason this dialogue is so polyvalent, the reason that texts are only partially determinate, the reason medieval multeity needs to be asserted against the modern monist fiction, is that human experience itself is often complex, undetermined, contradictory, and ambiguous. The appearance of unity conveyed by a text is merely a mask concealing the gaps in meaning, aporias, ideological lacunæ, fractures and fissures separating one intertextual voice from another, friction-points at the nexes of these intertexts where ideology butts up against ideology, where meaning conflicts with meaning. If this is true of literature written since the invention of print and the standardization of the textual surface, it is much more so in the case of medieval literature composed by frequently anonymous authors and preserved in a vast array of manuscripts by equally anonymous scribes in a variety of national, cultural, and local traditions whose relationship with the vestiges of the old Empire and/or Church of Rome can only be conceived in terms of the fallible human condition: people have always been partly submissive, partly rebellious, at times implacable and at times at peace with the authorities of government, school, and Church.

If a semiotic approach to medieval narrative replaces a work-immanent concept with intertextuality, it also replaces an Aristotelian notion of plot unity with narratological principles based more accurately on narrative structures inherent in medieval narratives themselves. As a consequence, the older conception of the task of the literary critic as one of close reading is altered as the focus of attention shifts away from the microstructures of the text—that is, the morphological and the lexical—toward larger discourse-structures in the texts. This may not be as radical a shift as it at first appears: the medieval New Critic performing a close reading of a text approaches the medieval text with much the same awareness of the manifold subcodes preconditioning the production of the text as the medievalist-semiotician. Political and religious history and scholastic philosophy and theology have always offered substantial insights into the thematic and even structural concerns of medieval literature. And philology, with its focus on the rich semantic subtleties exploited in the literary use of the medieval lexicon was not very far from the philosophy of language Umberto Eco has outlined in his recent *Semiotics and the Philosophy of Language*, where the restrictive "dictionary" meanings of language that come down through the Porphyrian tradition are rejected in favor of the "encyclopedic" understanding of semiotic structures that has been a major theme of Eco's work over the last ten years. Medievalists have always realized what Eco promotes as a concession to the lexicographic fixation: that the dictionary is only a tool [Eco (b): 84ff].

Embracing the alterity of medieval textuality

The modern medievalist's embracing of the alterity of medieval textuality entails several fundamental steps away from the mimetic textual tradition dominant during the last century and a half. The first involves a shift of focus away from the diachronic or historical approach to medieval language and literature to the synchronic. As any student of the history of thought in this century already no doubt knows, the importance of the distinction between these two axes in the study of language was asserted originally by Ferdinand de Saussure, whose *Course in General Linguistics* precipitated a rift between historical and structural linguistics and whose effects we still feel today. The force of reactionary criticism against structural linguistics that rests its case on a perceived failure to take historical succession into account; however this objection may be defused by valorizing Roman Jakobson's dynamic conception of synchrony, one which— developed early in his career and articulated again and again throughout—purposefully revises that of Saussure's before him not as a "homonomous unity" but one exhibiting both static *and* dynamic factors (Holenstein: 28). What is the source of this dynamism? Jakobson identifies it in the teleological orientation of both the synchronic and the diachronic axes, suggesting that "it is not an objective simultaneity, but the subjective experience of simultaneity that counts" (ibid.). Although we may (and in fact *must*) temporarily adopt the perspective of synchrony in forming a structural analysis of textual phenomenon, we nonetheless do so within a diachronic process and invest even the most atemporal elements of structural categories with temporality. In order to understand this more clearly, we must adduce a second Saussurian dichotomy, one that in general is less well-known outside the structural study of language: that of the syntagmatic versus the paradigmatic. This dichotomy bears certain resemblances to the difference between the synchronic and diachronic, as follows. If we think of a linguistic utterance or a literary text synchronically, we see all its various elements as occurring simultaneously without respect to its diachronic aspect—the changes it has gone or may undergo in time and its relationship to other utterances or texts coming before or following after it: we see, in a word, a "schematic" of its structure. Now the constituent elements of this schematic, in turn, may be seen in two ways: as *syntagms*—i.e., as contiguous units in a linear structure; and as manifestations of *paradigms*, or sets of related concepts united by means of association. For Saussure, the ideal type of the syntagm is the sentence, but he illustrates the difference between syntagmatic and paradigmatic by saying that

> ...a linguistic unit is like a fixed part of a building, e.g., a column. On the one hand, the column has a certain relation to the architrave it supports; the arrangement of the two units in space suggests the syntagmatic relations. On the other hand, if the column is Doric, it suggests a mental comparison of this style with others (Ionic, Corinthian, etc.) although none of these elements is present in space: the relation is associative.

Louis Hjelmslev was later to rename Saussure's associative relation as "paradigmatic," and this pair of concepts has been of great use in the structural analysis of all manner of linguistic and nonlinguistic phenomena by Lévi-Strauss, Barthes, and others. The relationship between units in a paradigm is synchronic—all members of the set are mutually present simultaneously—but dynamic: in the production of a text or an utterance, the choice of one as opposed to another member of a paradigmatic set is executed on the basis of the specialized meaning the text-producer wishes to convey at that point, and on the basis of the shades of difference that distinguish one member of the set from another.

The application of this dichotomy of perspectives has been used in the analysis of medieval literary texts in a turn toward the study of larger discourse-structures that has been undertaken largely—but not exclusively—under the ægis of the quasi-semiotic disciplines of textlinguistics, psycholinguistics, and stylistics. These disciplines are on the margins of literary semiotics in general and at the forefront of what Alexander Schwartz in 1983 called the "revival of philology." The new paradigm of medieval semiotic studies—whatever else distinguishes it—thus seems to involve a shift in focus away from a strictly lexical approach to medieval texts that was a hallmark of the New Critical movement in medieval studies half a century ago and toward discourse structures at a larger level. Other features of the paradigm, as I have suggested above, will no doubt involve the erasure of a rigid distinction between the synchronic and the diachronic in the study of medieval texts that Peter Haidu has seen as having a crippling effect upon medieval studies in this century (Haidu). Semiotics has much to teach medieval studies; the reverse of this is undoubtedly true as well, and the result of the convergence of these two fields promises to overcome at last the sometimes bitter dichotomy between historical and structural linguistics and, as a consequence, between philological and structuralist and post-structuralist conceptions of textuality. It is also likely to call into question the uncritical acceptance of the older hermeneutics and form-critical traditions as the be-all and end-all of the medieval scholarly enterprise.

The second step in embracing medieval textual alterity involves a critique of the conception of the literary work of art as the discrete product of an individual author, the product of an idiosyncratic vision—i.e., a "work-immanent" [Jauss (b): 78] view of literary ontology which is only part of the legacy of Renaissance and early Modern literary history:

> The humanistic model of classical texts also makes the book into a "work," a unique product of its creator. Certain basic distinctions follow from this which are as self-evident for the autonomous art of the bourgeois period as they are inappropriate for the medieval understanding of literature: the distinction between purposefulness and purposelessness, didactic and fictional, traditional and individual, imitative and creative. Medieval literature is a literature whose texts did not arise from the classical (and, later, Romantic) unity of author and work ... [Jauss (a): 188]

The recognizing of medieval textuality along the lines hinted at by Jauss occurs historically at the end of something like a century-and-a-half of research in medieval language, literature, history, and culture that has seen tremendous achievements leading to the uncritical reception of a concept of literary textuality preeminently amenable to university curricula but perhaps not to the nature of medieval textuality inself.

Intertextuality

Used as a heuristic and as something of a corrective to the monistic concept of textuality implicit in the history of philological criticism just summarized, the concept of *intertextuality*—introduced in European criticism by Julia Kristeva and popularized ty Roland Barthes and others—is analogous in many respects to Mikhail Bakhtin's dialogic principle. According to this view of the literary work, a text is not created *ex nihilo* but rather represents a "mirage de citations" (Barthes), a patchwork of allusions, quotations, and references that in one way or another reconstitutes a vast network of texts in a new concatenation that itself will serve at a later point as just another strand to be interwoven in a new combination of textual utterances.

This is where semiotics comes in, with a radically different conception—not only of textuality itself, but also of the status of texts in the entire system of signification that comprise coherent culture, a system whose complexity is provocatively captured under Even-Zohar's 1979 label of "polysystem." The semioticization of medieval studies is changing the ways in which we conceive of texts. For an interesting summary of the impact of some of these theoretical and methodological developments specifically on medieval studies, I would refer you to Alexander Schwartz's 1983 article. But among all these, in the sphere of research properly represented by the term "semiotics," one element of the emerging paradigm is that of "intertextuality," introduced in modern critical debate by Mikhail Bakhtin, a Russian critical theorist and historian of the novel who wrote throughout the middle of this century and died in Moscow in 1975. The *term* "intertextuality" apparently was coined by the European literary theorist Julia Kristeva in the early 1970's under the direct influence of Bakhtin's writings, which at that time were available only in Russian; Bakhtin's major works have since been made known to English-speaking students by his principal translators Helene Iswolsky and J. Michael Holquist.

When using the concept of "intertextuality," modern literary theorists do not mean merely that authors quote one another. This is, of course, part of the idea, but there is rather a different fundamental conception of the text that is offered by this term. The concept of intertextuality in the fullest sense of its denotation means that not only do authors quote each other, but they also quote themselves; they quote authors in genres different from their own, and they quote non-authors, and such quotation is inevitable as it is often done unconsciously. Further, authors inevitably *mis*quote the material they use, thereby producing accidental parodies and perpetuating downright errors—often in the very act of trying to promote forthright truth. Even the wholehearted attempt to quote faithfully introduces a quoted text to a new *context*, with an attendant hermeneutic shift that must be taken into account in the act of interpretation—one cannot walk into the same river twice; a new context creates a new text. As Kristeva has said:

> Dans cette perspective nour définissons LE TEXTE comme un appareil translinguistique qui redistribue l'ordre de la langue, en mettant en relation une parole communicative visant l'information directe, avec differents types d'énoncés antérieurs ou synchroniques. Le texte est donc une PRODUCTIVITE, ce qui veut dire: (1) son rapport à la langue dans laquelle il se situe est redistributif ... ; (2) il est une permutation de textes, une inter-textualité: dans l'espace d'un texte plusieurs énoncés, pris à d'autres textes, se croisent et se neutralisent. (Kristeva: 12)[2]

Kristeva derived this concept from Bakhtin, who metaphorized this phenomenon, describing a network of texts as a chorus of voices meeting in a dialogue, sometimes cacophonous, none of them enjoying any special priority, all of them being subject to centripetal and centrifugal forces pulling at one moment toward convention and at another moment pulling toward innovation. Bakhtin speaks of the *polyglossia* (Bakhtin: 61) of the world's languages; *heteroglossia* within any given language; and the *dialogic* characteristics of a given text:

> Every concrete utterance of a speaking subject serves as a point where centrifugal as well as centripetal forces are brought to bear. The processes of centralization and decentralization, of

unification and disunification, intersect in the utterance; the utterance not only answers the requirements of its own language as an individualized embodiment of a speech act, but it answers the requirements of *heteroglossia* as well; it is in fact an active participant in such speech diversity. And this active participation of every utterance in living *heteroglossia* determines the linguistic profile and style of the utterance to no less a degree than its inclusion in any normative-centralizing system of a unitary language. (Bakhtin: 272)

Bakhtin characterizes medieval literature in particular as follows:

The relationship to another's word was equally complex and ambiguous in the Middle Ages. The role of the other's word was enormous at that time: there were quotations that were openly and reverently emphasized as such, or that were half-hidden, completely hidden, half-conscious, unconscious, correct, intentionally distorted, unintentionally distorted, deliberately reinterpreted and so forth. The boundary lines between someone else's speech and one's own speech were flexible, ambiguous, often deliberately distorted and confused. Certain types of texts were constructed like mosaics out of the texts of others. (Bakhtin: 69)

But of course we recognize that if the concept of intertextuality is accepted in the widest sense of the term, not only "certain types of texts" but indeed all texts are constructed out of other texts like mosaics. The extent to which priority of voice is perceived by its audience is merely the result of the "author"/moderator's attempt to structure this dialogue according to some privileged, *monoglossic* language combined with the audience's own post-production tendency to do the same. Hence the importance of the history of a text's *reception* as a key to the history of its meanings—a point that has been made quite convincingly by Hans Robert Jauss.

Of course, the dynamics of this intertextual dialogue are constantly changing; hence, in recent critical theory, the disappearance of a speaking subject in narrative; hence the emergence of a point of view reflected in such statements as the Heideggerian "it is no longer I who speak, but language that speaks through me," with the concomitant privileging of *langue* over *parole* in linguistics beginning with Saussure and including his more recent advocates Louis Hjelmslev and Roland Barthes among many others. This understanding of textuality has implications in three major respects for medieval studies: intertextuality can be seen as a characteristic of (1) the structure of individual texts including, in a major way, *narrative* structure; (2) the relationships between manuscripts in a family of associated texts; and (3) the recycling of language at all levels of discourse across genres, manuscript families, and individual texts.

PART TWO: THE MANUSCRIPT LABYRINTH AND THE SCHOLARLY EDITION

A variety of implications concerning our conceptions of medieval authors and their work, orality versus literacy, Latin versus vernacular language and poetics, and structural units in medieval texts could result from these theoretical considerations; however, the most important insight has to do with the problematic conception of medieval "works" of literature as opposed to the relatively unproblematical status of *manuscripts* in the study of medieval literature. The most important implication for the shift of perspective we are here remarking would be at least curricular and pedagogical. The understanding of the intertextual character of medieval literature that is fostered in the semiotic approach allows us to put manuscripts back in the center of our perception of where the texts of medieval literature lie rather than to accept uncritically the decisions of a generation of textual editors whose labors have *given us the very materials* upon which we now have the privilege to operate in reading, interpreting, teaching and writing about the literature of the Middle Ages. As Jerome J. McGann and a number of others have been pointing out recently, textual-editorial work has been relegated increasingly to something like a "Restricted Area" of scholarly endeavor, with the result, sadly, that many graduate programs in medieval studies contain no component for orthographic, paleographic, or manuscript instruction, nor even the opportunity for such work. The fact is that some medieval studies programs reinforce the modern devaluation of manuscripts, leaving it up to the individual—and generally only at the post-doctoral or early profesional stage—to fill the gap on his or her own.

To medievalists, this all sounds rather familiar, and not very surprising: we have known for a long time that if literary activity can be charted along a continuum ranging from pure convention to pure artistic creativity—between design and design, tradition and innovation, *koine* and idiolect—medieval literature tends toward the first of these two extremes. Many of the writers whose texts we read, teach, and write about saw their craft as being at its best when it was able artistically to rearrange, reuse, and reconstitute earlier texts as opposed to creating altogether new ones. The loss of the speaking subject in modern theory is nothing new to us since the self-effacement of many of these writers was achieved with total success in many cases, and we know nothing of the identity or personality of the author responsible for many medieval works. The degree to which modern literary theory has accorded primacy to *system* as opposed to the uniqueness of person, utterance, and intention, is directly analogous to the extent to which many medieval texts appear to be manifestations of a literary or cultural system—a chorus of competing voices—rather than the unique product of an authorial personality at a particular place in space and time.

Now there is a curious paradox in all this: a great deal of the energy in medieval studies has been and continues to be devoted to textual editing that aims to establish the *authoritative* text for a given "work" of literature. Ironically, given the lack of traceable authorship for much medieval literature, we have chosen to accord authoritative status to particular *editions* or in some cases to specific *manuscripts* of medieval texts. In Old English, for example, we speak of the Klaeber edition of *Beowulf* , recognizing as we do so that the text of *Beowulf* as Klaeber presents it is unmistakably the creation of Klaeber himself, a creation based (we hope) upon sound editorial judgments and years of meticulous scholarship. Sometimes, indeed, we refer to this edition simply as "Klaeber." It is only recently that this situation has been challenged wholesale, in the work of Kevin Kiernan and (somewhat more radically) Raymond P. Tripp, whose divergent (and quite different) responses to the problems they see in the uncritical reception of the standard editions may not in all cases garner unqualified support but at least give us pause to reflect upon the nature of our acceptance.

At any rate, the notion of intertextuality that is most familiar to medievalists is probably that which obtains in the phenomenon of variant manuscripts of a particular work. Here we meet with the problem in a different form, since the work of establishing an authoritative edition for a given text involves the selection of one voice among the chorus authorizing it to speak for the rest, who fade into the background of *stammbaumen*, *sigilla*, alphabetic codes at the bottom of the page, textual notes in the appendices of a text in smaller-point type, or mere mentions in the front matter. How many rival texts have been effectively shut-up in modern editions with phrases such as "not in E," or "*vide* folio MS 489," or "lacuna in Harley MS"? We have effectively shifted authority of author to that of edition, and have gone on to treat the intertextuality of medieval texts as if it were not very important.

The dominant model informing the editing of medieval texts has emphasized genetic relations between sources, in an elevation of the historical principle to the status of absolute rule, a rule whose negative articulation takes the following form: "If we know not whence a thing comes, we know it not" (Darwin). The sources of the operative model informed by this rule are manifold, and a specific theory of textuality lies behind this model, a theory that I think conflicts radically with the theory of textuality inherent in the medieval culture it has been used to elucidate. As a result of the lack of a proper fit between medieval textuality and the theory of textuality implicit in modern editing of medieval texts, a poor understanding of medieval literature has been fostered from the time of the neogrammarians until the end of the New Critical tradition in our own time. The unique task of semiotics may well lie in its ability to demythologize the dominant tradition in medieval studies, or at least bring underlying theoretical assumptions to the surface so that they can be evaluated and, if necessary, be redefined. Among these I think it is essential to scrutinize the editorial tradition in medieval studies.

This critique occurs historically during a decisive period of adjustment in which "[t]extual criticism is in the process of reconceiving its discipline" [McGann (a): 2] in which scholarly projects devoted to the discovery of "lost original documents" have been "thrown into a state of general scholarly crisis" [McGann (a): 4].

The larger problem which verges on semiotic principles has to do with just what commodity should be considered the textual object, and this problem impinges upon the study of medieval literature, whose poetics of alterity has been described by modern critical theorists as being radically at variance with both classical mimetic and traditional modern poetics. Such theorists as Paul Zumthor, Peter Haidu, Hans Robert Jauss, and Eugene Vance have demonstrated rather cogently that medieval literary tradition really has more in common with postmodern poetic theory and practice than with its predecessors in ancient Greek and Latin poetics. Likewise, medieval poetics has less in common with its successors in the modern tradition, which draws upon a mimeticism whose hegemony in European culture went practically unchallenged from its inception in the Renaissance until sometime during this century. As far as prose narratives go, such postmodern genres as surfiction and metafiction may in fact offer closer parallels to the medieval understanding of linguistic and poetic structure than anything else we are likely to find in less recent literary practice.

The highly intertextual character of medieval literature is the salient feature in its alterity, the "éloignement du moyen âge, la distance irrécuperable qui nous en sépare" (Zumthor), explaining its difference not only from classical and modern mimeticism but also helping to explain its difference from itself—that is, the propensity for literary texts to draw from many sources simultaneously, weaving a fabric whose æsthetic appeal lies not so much in its openness to the reader's "self-submersion in the unique world of a single work" but rather in its intertextuality, demanding that the reader "negate the character of the individual text as a work in order to enjoy the charm of an already ongoing game with known rules and still unknown surprises" [Jauss (a): 189]. This intertextual quality "presupposes an expectation which can only be fulfilled by the step from text to text, for here the pleasure is provided by the perception of difference, of an ever-different variation on a basic pattern" (ibid.). This phenomenon, the "step from text to text," has implications in the episodic structure of medieval prose narratives (Haidu, Evans), which exhibit an overall pattern that we can hardly call a "plot" in the Aristotelian sense, and which borrow episodes wholesale from other texts. It also helps to explain the relationship between manuscripts in a corpus in a way that enables the differences between them to be treated not as a problem to be eliminated in editorial handling but rather as part of the ongoing history of the development of a text even after it has left the hands of what we might in traditional terms call the "original author."

The problem with editions of medieval texts is that the modern critical edition tends to silence the intertextual chorus with a modern "work-immanent" conception of the literary text and thus to disguise the highly allusive nature of medieval poetics. This comes out in the way the standard critical edition treats the manuscripts, arranging them in a hierarchy of value judged from the standpoint of their presumed relation to the original form the text exhibited at the moment of its creation. This quest for origins defines the manuscript-editorial process and at the same time defines the larger political and cultural goals that have quietly supported some medieval studies projects—quietly, even invisibly, in a scholarly project that has often presented itself in objective, positivist, scientific terms as if it could be divorced from such underpinning.

Within the global medieval studies community, medieval French and Middle English literary/critical theorists have undertaken a shift toward the semiotic perspective somewhat earlier than scholars in other national/cultural traditions have, most notably Old English and Old Norse—and the whole Germanic branch of medieval studies remains curiously hide-bound. However, there is some evidence of a growing recognition of the value of newer perspectives, which have been seen as "generating heat and light" (Joseph Harris) and as promising to "breathe new life into more conventional methods such as the close comparison of manuscript-versions and textual variants" (Joseph Harris: 9). In the analysis and criticism of Old Norse saga narratives, for example, new methods drawn from anthropology, folklore methodology, and so on—the disciplines touched earliest by structuralism and semiotics—have been recognized by medievalists in Scandinavian studies as helping to elucidate a "semiotic grammar which we find hard to understand" by virtue of its alterity (ibid.). The use of modern semiotics to formalize this grammar would further help to objectify the "differing authorial intentions" implicit in variant manuscripts, which "thus may be seen as representing 'two' or 'three' sagas, rather than just the textual deterioration of 'one' saga (ibid.)."

The Stammbaum paradigm

The dominant paradigm in the editing of medieval manuscripts which we must investigate in the remainder of this essay is just that manuscript-editorial paradigm which enables critics to identify manuscript sources as "pure" and their copies as "deteriorated" or "corrupt" and thus to denigrate their status as objective signs.

The immediate source behind this practice is to be found in the neogrammarian movement of the 1860's, whereby literary colleagues of Karl Lachmann, Wilhelm and Friedrich von Schlegel, Andreas Heusler, and Jakob Grimm extended Sir William Jones' and Franz Bopp's Indo-European hypothesis to the editorial handling of manuscripts. The neogrammarians, interestingly enough, took a number of theoretical/methodological cues from the natural sciences—botany, zoology, and even geology (Christy) having experienced a relatively precipitous paradigm-shift textualized in 1859 in Charles Darwin's *Origin of Species*. The new paradigm centered upon a synthetic view of chronological succession developed by Hegel, and it expressed itself—in the natural sciences, in linguistics, and in textual criticism—in the form of a taxonymous genealogical chart. The relations between plants, animals, human languages, and manuscripts were drawn along the lines of a hierarchically-structured model emphasizing dichotomies in a genetic process of development from *genus*, or source, to *species*, or thing-in-itself. August Schleicher is among the earliest among the neogrammarians to have done this with the Indo-European languages. Schleicher, who was not a professional linguist, records his debt to Darwinian biology in the very title of his work: *Die Darwinische Theorie und die Sprachwissenschaft* , and the result of his efforts was the genealogical table of languages which has proven to be so successful that many standard dictionaries of English still publish some version of it somewhere in their flyleaves.

Botany had a profound influence on both late 19th-century linguistics and textual editing. August Schleicher was a botanist, not a professional philologist, and his progressivist linguistics predated the influence of Darwin upon him. Without a doubt, it was the hierarchical system of organizing plants developed by the Swedish botanist Linnæus (we all remember the incantation "kingdom, phylum, class, order, family, genus, species" from school) that profoundly influenced his linguistics.

It was a fellow Swede, Carl Johan Schlyter, who first used the *stemma* to articulate *manuscript* relations in his edition of the *Vestgotalagen* in 1927 (Holm), and, like Schleicher's genealogical table of Indo-European languages, it was so successful as to be adopted as the only acceptable model for describing the textual relations of manuscript sources for the rest of the century and all of this one. The model is implicit, it is accepted uncritically, and rarely has it been critically considered by medievalists (but see McGann and Haugen).

Indeed, the *stemma* is central to Paul Maas's *Testkritik* which is the definitive—and practically the *only*—theoretical and programmatic treatment of manuscript relations currently used in the preparation of scholarly editions—as, for example, in the Arnamagnæn Institute in Copenhagen, which for two hundred and fifty years has authoritatively set the course for editing medieval Scandinavian texts. Maas states the goal of scholarly editing unequivocally: "The business of textual criticism is to produce a text as close as possible to the original" (Maas: 1). The model guiding Maas is that of the *stemma*: "The image," he says, "is taken from genealogy: the witnesses are related to the original somewhat as the descendants of a man are related to their ancestor." Maas goes on to make the odious statement that "One might perhaps illustrate the transmission of errors along the same lines by treating all females as sources of error" (Maas: 20), and he goes further to use the simile of a flowing river to describe the "transmission of errors" upon which so much depends in his textual/editorial process, which he also likens to historiographical concerns, folklore research, and the kind of literary source criticism which has been something of a *sine qua non* in our own field for quite some time.

Maas points to similarities between the *stemma* and the branching relations between streams and river-beds, and analogizes the process of textual criticism as one of testing various outlets of underground streams for "contaminants" which must be eliminated in the process of identifying the pure source from which the water flows. Indeed, error and contamination are of great significance in the construction of a stemma, as "the ideal procedure is to undertake a word by word collation of all the manuscripts in question. Correspondence between manuscripts is, however, of less interest than deviations, particularly shared deviations. The stemmatic investigation thus concentrates on the telling mistakes and common blunders in order to rank the manuscripts in a final stemma" (Haugen: 428).

Where such a model goes wrong lies *not in the hierarchical nature of the model, but in the application of the dynamic element, and specifically in its teleology*. "The consensus on the model does not entail consensus on the rules for its construction. Hard and fast rules simply do not exist" (Haugen: 438). In fact, the apparent origins of the stemma in Linnæan botany—which was evolutionary in the progressivist sense, not in the atavistic sense of retrograde metamorphosis—suggest an orientation *downward*, if you will, in the hierarchy, with the genetic possibilities encoded higher in the hierarchy most fully realized and articulated in organisms at the level of the *species*. In the Linnæan scheme, things at the *specific* level are most fully themselves; the genetic mutations that produce species are not degenerations *away from* some perfect generic or phyletic original but rather mutations *toward* something that is complete in its self-immanence.

But the ways editors of medieval texts have treated the manuscripts of medieval "works of literature" reveals a retrospective orientation, and the process of development in a manuscript tradition is seen as entropic rather than as the reverse; the goal of textual criticism and textual editing has been to clear away verbal clutter in seeking the *original* form of the text—on this point, Maas is quite unambiguous—but I would ask the question "why?" The answer is self-evident only if we assume that the original is somehow preferable to the extant copies. This is not always the case.

The source of potential error in the use of the stemma lies in its application, not in the model itself. The manner in which it has been applied privileges the oral over the written, valorizes the presence of the speaking subject, and perpetuates the mythic significance of the originary moment of enunciation, all of which are the legacy of Western semiotics launched in Christianity, developed in Augustine's verbal epistemology (Colish), and deconstructed in our own era by Jacques Derrida. Stemmatic evidence furnishes material with which the textual critic can define the shape of the first written witness in a manuscript corpus. But it does not enable him thereby to approach the moment of the manuscript's original creation when its meaning was invested, and thus the key to the text's power to signify lies behind an unbreachable barrier, inviolable by even the most rigorous of linguistic scientific methods.

This has not prevented medieval textual editors from crossing the barrier, however. As Frantzen and Venegoni have pointed out, Karl Lachmann's edition of the *Nibelungenlied* did just that— moved backward beyond the first manuscript of the work to the moment of its origin. Similarly, Andreas Heusler, working with great confidence from extant manuscripts, had to define and name at least five absent texts in his effort to write the history of the sources of the *Volsunga saga*, *Prose Edda*, and *Nibelungenlied* (Anderson).

The specific claims advanced by Lachmann and Heusler must be taken seriously and not summarily dismissed. But it seems clear that stemmatic methodology irresistably tempts its users to apply theoretical principles beyond their self-inscribed limitation so that the hidden origins of a text can appear to present themselves for analysis just as accessibly as the extant manuscripts do, by a scientific process that disguises its inherently magical qualities. Lachmann and Heuslers' work developed the mythic origins of Germanic heroism in a period of our century when such origins served as justification for large-scale political and military endeavors whose results we know only too well—all in the name of the objective, scientific study of language in literature.

The stemma uses the metaphor of the branching structure of trees to explain genetic relationships between manuscripts. This metaphor serves as a heuristic model, borrowed from Linnæan botany in the neogrammarian account of the relation between Indo-European languages and in the science of etymology which is intimately connected with the neogrammarian enterprise: etymology and lexicography go hand in hand, and the monumental results of such work are still to be seen in the great dictionaries of the national languages and their linguistic precursors. The nationalism inherent in these great cultural projects is unmistakable. Frantzen and Venegoni have brilliantly unearthed some of the nationalistic preoccupations acting programmatically in the German sources of Anglo-Saxon studies; one only has to read the account of J.A.H. Murray's career while working on the *Oxford English Dictionary* (Murray) to see how the preparation of that dictionary was dependent upon the sustaining efforts of the hundreds of loyal English citizens who prepared the millions of slips on a volunteer basis; one also sees connections between the nationalistic spirit supporting the *OED* and those of the Early English Text Society, published to provide grist for the lexicographic mill; and one sees further the connection between these projects and the other editorial and scholarly projects upon which all the subsequent history of Anglo-Saxon studies has been based—the preparation of Old English grammars, dictionaries, critical editions, and all the attendant linguistic- and literary-critical debate swirling round them.

In Scandinavian studies, one finds much the same thing: the genealogical principle giving birth to dictionaries and critical editions and nations or national myths all at the same time. The manuscript materials that have served as the foundation for the tremendous scholarly industry of medieval Scandinavian studies were gathered in the late 17th and early 18th centuries during a period of fierce national competition for medieval cultural artefacts between Denmark and Sweden, whose scholarly and diplomatic representatives roamed the mountains and fjords of Norway and the forbidding volcanic landscape of Iceland for manuscripts that would help southern Scandinavia to document its origins, and Sweden and Denmark fought bitterly over these materials. The history of the disposition of the manuscripts at the center of this activity is one filled with scholarly intrigue, stolen manuscripts and libraries, catastrophic fires, and so on. Late in the Renaissance these manuscripts had become so devalued in cultural terms that when they came to the attention of the Icelander Arne Magnusson, professor in the University of Copenhagen from 1709–1732, they were being systematically discarded, cut up into pieces as book-bindings or as stiffeners for eccesiastical headwear or—in at least one case—for garment patterns (Hermannsson).

The status of these manuscripts as signs of the political and cultural movements of the time may be seen through an interpretive reading of the catalogues of these manuscripts. The catalogue of the manuscripts collected reveals the following pattern: legal and historiographic texts, in general, are indexed first—with corresponding manuscript *numbers*—in the folio, quarto, and octavo sections of the collection, with religious materials coming next, and literary romances and other trivial matters coming toward the end. The current disposition of these manuscripts further illustrates these manuscripts' status as cultural-historical artefacts: the Arnamagnæan manuscripts are housed in a vault six layers in from the street--one has to pass through *six* doors from Njalsgade on the island of Amager in Copenhagen to actually get to the manuscripts—six layers of corridors, hallways, reading-rooms, and so forth, the last two barricades being tended by manuscript guardians who wear keys around their necks to unlock the last door and the vault. And of course the University buildings themselves attest to the relative cultural value placed upon these manuscripts and all the intellectual activity that surrounds them—I am reminded of a passage in David Lodge's *Small World*:

> They [Persse McGarigle and Morris Zapp] had reached a summit which offered a panoramic view of Rummidge University … . "See what I mean?" [Zapp] panted, with an all-embracing, yet dismissive sweep of his arm. "It's huge, heavy, monolithic. It weighs about a billion tons. You can *feel* the weight of those buildings, pressing down the earth. Look at the Library—built like a huge warehouse. The whole place says, *'We have learning stored here; if you want it, you've got to come inside and get it.'*

I am not sure how seriously we must take Zapp's further consideration that the hoarding of information is no longer necessary or desirable and that three things have revolutionized academic life in the last quarter-century—telephones, jet travel, and xerox machines—but I am reminded of a maxim passed on to me by a Viennese scholar of Old Norse: "*Kopieren geht über studieren*," which probably should be revised into closer proximity with the truth—*Kopieren IST studieren*.

It is only the result of a whole series of prior judgments that renders the value of manuscripts perfectly sensible, since these manuscripts are absolutely priceless—in *cultural terms*. This is important: cultures by their very nature invest power in systems of self-aggrandizement and self-perpetuation and they must use and dispense language in a way that serves this self-protective end. The copying and preservation of a manuscript is far from a simple chirographic or bibliographic fact. And of course even these valorative gestures say nothing of the meaning invested through the subsequent activities of collating, transcribing, editing, publishing, analysis, criticism, interpretation, translation, and so on that represent the latter stages in the reception-historical trajectory of a piece of medieval literature.

A good number of the manuscripts that resided in the Arnamagnæan Institute in Copenhagen from the institute's inception in the early 18th century until the last two decades are medieval, vellum manuscripts dating from the 13th through the 16th centuries. Many of them, though, are "only" paper copies of vellum manuscripts—some now lost—made during a great wave of Icelandic nationalism and humanistic renaissance in the 17th and 18th centuries fostered at a distance by the 19th century nationalistic upsurge in southern Scandinavia. Their continuing status in political history is shown by their disposition even in this era. Once Iceland won full independence from Denmark in the last 1940's, Iceland demanded the return of their cultural legacy, which they claimed—with a great deal of truth—had been taken from them unjustly three hundred years ago. Denmark was surprisingly sympathetic to this claim, with the result that in 1972, surrounded by great diplomatic fanfare, welcoming committees, etc., the Codex Regius of the *Elder* Edda was returned to Iceland, with some 1100 manuscripts to follow over the next decade. Manuscripts thus continue to exert an influence on the genealogy of texts as well as on the genealogy of nations.

Both natural and linguistic science in the 18th and 19th centuries appear to have used the genealogical model whose ultimate origin is to be found in the Porphyrian tree. In the third century, Porphyry of Tyre "systematized the doctrine of the [Aristotelian] predicables enumerating five types [of predicable]: genus, specific differences, species, property, and accident," which was a basic logical and epistemological tool later in the middle ages (Bochenski: 134). Porphyry developed at once an extensional view of terms and a system of classification based on differences between genus and species, which later was to be used in the medieval art of grammatical definition and, later still, in constructing a hierarchical model based on difference, which is the fundamental tool used in textual criticism to distinguish between exemplars and copies in a group of related manuscripts. But the important factor we should note here is that Porphyry's tree, developed in a text introducing the Aristotelian Categories, explains the difference between genus and species on the basis of Aristotle's dichotomy between substance and accidence, with the dominant, valorized term in *substance*, correlated by Porphyry with a *genus*, and with species in the secondary position correlated with Aristotle's *accidence*. "The common genus, 'what is', has nothing over it. It is the beginning of things and everything is inferior to it.... Genus is what is predicated essentially (en to ti esti), of several things differing in species" (Bochenski: 136). The practical effect of the application of this model is to reduce all species to a subordinate role in relation to genus, and the end result of the application of this model to manuscript relations is to reduce the signifying status of copies except perhaps in the mere indexical sense of pointing backward to their exemplars—the genus, in Porphyrian terms, which generated them. Exemplars have meaningful status; exemplars *signify*. Copies have significant status only insofar as they stand for exemplars.

But manuscripts are real objects, the product of a whole web of specific cultural and personal motivations—a manuscript, in my view, ought never to be reduced to the status of a "mere" copy, however "corrupt" it may be judged to be in relation to some idea of pure originality. In Old English, for example, Kevin Kiernan advanced the thesis in his controversial *Beowulf and the Beowulf Manuscript* that the poem originates precisely with the creation of the manuscript, which he sees as conjoining two different pre-existing texts about the poem's hero in a unique text coexistent with its manuscript.

In Old Icelandic studies, there is a distinction made between decorative manuscripts versus those written for common use. Some of these, religious ones in particular and the many many copies of *Jónsbók*, the Norwegian revision of Icelandic law sponsored by King Magnus of Norway and adopted in Iceland by the Althing in 1282, are beautiful works of art, evidencing a tremendous amount of labor expended on them as texts and as objects. These were no doubt underwritten by royal patronage— the medieval equivalent of a modern research grant. Others, more often literary texts, far more humble in provenance, barely present their texts in legible form, many of them being further obscured by the accumulation of centuries of grime and smoke from usage in monastic libraries and in the homes of wealthy farmers and landholders. Monastic manuscripts seem especially subject to tampering by their copyists, and the margins of many of the ones I've seen are filled with scrawled phrases and sentences such as "GuD hjalpe mer," ("God help Me,") and invocations of the trinity and the blessed virgin—prayers no doubt formed on the lips and in the styluses of scribes bored by the endless and unspeakably tedious chore of copying out script. And even in the least decorative of manuscripts one frequently finds doodled drawings of people and animals, sometimes totally unrelated to the subject-matter of the central text, other times making apparent commentary on the texts whose margins they fill.

This may seem trivial, but the point is that each extant manuscript by its very existence is inscribed by a motive to preserve and to pass on, and attests to a range of motives at the intersection not only of the stemmatic evidence and the history of a particular "work," but also of personal, institutional, cultural, political and religious systems, even animal husbandry. I cannot begin to estimate the number of head of livestock who gave their lives to produce the vellum on which most of what we know about the middle ages could be preserved—a paschal sacrifice of tremendous importance in the sacred history of our profession.

Mapping the Manuscript Hierarchy

It is perhaps truer to the holistic nature of the medieval manuscript as semiotic object—that is, as the produce of human semiosis or the human effort to employ signs as vehicles of meaning—to take as our starting-point a perspective on manuscript that recognizes two components of the hierarchy: verbal and nonverbal. The verbal component obviously includes the language recorded in the center of the manuscript leaves as well as any extraneous language inscribed in the margins. The nonverbal component includes illuminations, marginal drawings, non-linguistic doodles, and other markings. Both are significant, and both must be "read" if we are to fully understand the manuscripts' full meaning. Actually, even this mapping of the hierarchy is somewhat cursory and overly generalized since any specific parchment encodes a great deal of information that may be overlooked by purely an editorial interest in constructing a stemma of textual relations while attempting to establish the "authoritative text of the work." For example, the vellum of any given manuscript suggests pertinent data ranging from medieval animal husbandry, the technical art of curing sheep- and calf-skins for the preparation of vellum; up to the size and opulence of the institution responsible for the creation of a codex. *Flateyarbók*, for example, a superb Icelandic folio manuscript, was a tremendously expensive project, requiring the slaughter of about 113 calves, a fact that says a great deal concerning the human valorization of the texts it preserves. I doubt that the calves themselves cared much for it. Manuscript marginalia—both verbal and pictorial—the "doodles" and the stray scraps of verbal graffiti—encode all kinds of information concerning scribal and readerly attitudes towards the texts central to them.

The chirographic component, also, has its own complex history, with elements of orthography borrowed early from Anglo-Saxon insular writing before the supersession of the Caroline minuscule, to western Norwegian scribal practice in and around Bergen in the eleventh century, with decidedly more Caroline influence. And the texts—the verbal texts—themselves are, as one would imagine, rich fields of intertextual nexation drawing together sources from the whole panorama of encyclopedic medieval learning gathered from Græco-Roman culture, Western and Eastern Christianity, Arabic science, and so on, including the indigenous Scandinavian cultures overspread by Roman culture, Greek philosophy, and Christian belief. And of course the artistic illustrations constitute a highly sophisticated language all their own.

Among the solutions to the present general crisis in textual editorial theory and methodology, Jerome J. McGann recommends first that we become "fully conscious" of the history of our own scholarly institutions and of the central role that textual criticism plans in literary studies. I would suggest that this crisis is especially pernicious in medieval studies, since the textual materials with which we are occupied—i.e., manuscripts—are relatively inaccessible, at least to North Americans, and we are therefore so utterly dependent upon the way these materials are mediated to us. And I suggest by way of conclusion that by virtue of its peculiar characteristics, semiotics stands in the best position to undertake the sort of critique we now envision.

NOTES

1. [The analysis of the texts and the codes that fail to appear at the surface of a given discourse but which at the same time have had a part in the process of production of the former, appears to be essential: their study can offer to us fundamental clarifications concerning the process of production itself and also concerning the understanding of discourse at the point of its reception.... . These hidden discourses (which one may compare to the blueprints and drawings of an architectural plan) play an instrumental role in the production of a certain discursive object and at the same time constitute a privileged place where certain ideological mechanisms transpire in the work of the production. These emerge, if one may

say it thus, from an intertextuality "in-depth", because they are the texts which, playing a part in the process of production of other texts, never arrive in and of themselves (or very rarely, or according to the canons of restraint) at the social consummation of discourse.]   [Veron, in Eco (a): 149].

2. [From this perspective we define the text as a translinguistic fabric that redistributes the order of the language, in placing a communicative word into a relationship with direct information, with different types of anterior or synchronic utterances. The text is thus a productivity, about which one can say (1) its relationship with the language in which it is situated is redistributive... ; (2) it is a permutation of texts, an intertextuality: in the space of a text, many utterances, extracted from other texts, cross upon each other and neutralize one another.]

REFERENCES

Anderson, Theodore M. 1980. *The Legend of Brynhild* . Islandica 43. Ithaca, N.Y.: Cornell University Press.

Bakhtin, Mikhail. 1981. *The Dialogic Imagination.* J. Michael Holquist, ed.; Caryl Emerson and J. Michael Holquist, trs. Austin: University of Texas Press.

Bloch, R. Howard. 1983. *Etymologies and Genealogies: A Literary Anthropology of the French Middle Ages.* Chicago: University of Chicago Press.

Bochenski, I.M. 1970. *A History of Formal Logic.* 2nd edition. New York: Chelsea.

Cederschiöld, Gustaf. 1884. *Konrads sage. Fornsögur Sudrlanda.* Lund: Berlings, 43-84.

Christy, T. Craig. *Uniformitarianism in Linguistics.* Amsterdam: John Benjamins.

Colish, Marcia L. 1983. *The Mirror of Language: A Study in the Medieval Theory of Knowledge.* 2nd ed. Lincoln: University of Nebraska Press.

Eco, Umberto. (a) 1976. *A Theory of Semiotics.* Bloomington: Indiana University Press.

————. (b) 1984. *Semiotics and the Philosophy of Language.* Bloomington: Indiana University Press.

Evans, Jonathan. 1987. "Medieval Studies and Semiotics: Perspectives on Research," *Semiotica* 67: 1/2.

Even-Zohar, Itamar. 1979. Polysystem theory. *Poetics Today* 1, 287-310.

Frantzen, Allen J. and Charles Venegoni. 1986. "An Archæology of Anglo-Saxon Studies," *Style* 20:2, 142-156.

Gunnlaugur Thordarsyni. 1859. *Konrads saga keisarasonar er for til ormalands.* Copenhagen: Møller.

Harris, Joseph. 1985. "Eddic Poetry." In *Old Norse-Icelandic Literature,* John Lindow and Carol J. Clover, eds. Islandica. Ithaca, N.Y.: Cornell University Press.

Harris, Richard L. "The Lion-knight Legend in Iceland and the Valthjolfstadir Door." *Viator* 1, 125-145.

Hermannsson, Halldór. 1929. *Icelandic Manuscripts.* Islandica 19. Ithaca, N.Y.: Cornell University Press. Rpt. Kraus 1967.

Haugen, Odd Einar. 1985. "The Evaluation of Stemmatic Evidence: Recension and Revision of Niörstigningar saga." *The Sixth International Saga Conference, Workshop Papers.* Det Arnamagnæan Institut, arr. Copenhagan: Det Arnamagnæanske Legat, 423-450.

Holenstein, Elmar. 1972. *Roman Jakobson's Approach to Language.* Bloomington, Indiana University Press.

Holm, Gosta. 1972. "Carl Johan Schlyter and Textual Scholarship." *Saga och Sed*, 48-80.

Jauss, Hans Robert. (a) 1979. "The Alterity and Modernity of Medieval Literature." *New Literary History* 10, 181-229.

—————. (b) 1982. *Toward an Æsthetic of Reception.* Tim Bahti, tr. Theory and History of Criticism, vol. 2. Minneapolis: University of Minnesota Press.

Kiernan, Kevin S. 1984. *Beowulf and the Beowulf Manuscript.* Hanover, N.H.: Rutgers University Press.

Kristeva, Julia. 1970. *Le Teste du roman.* The Hague: Mouton.

Kuhn, Thomas S. (a) 1972. *The structure of Scientific Revolutions.* 2nd ed. Chicago: University of Chicago Press. Lodge, David.

—————. (b) 1977. *The Essential Tension.* Chicago: University of Chicago Press.

Maas, Paul. *Textual Criticism.* Oxford: Oxford University Press.

McGann, Jerome J. (a) 1983. *A Critique of Modern Textual Criticism.* Chicago: University of Chicago Press.

—————. (b) 1985. "The Makers and the Giants: Textual and Bibliographical Studies and the Interpretation of Literary Works." In *Textual Criticism and Literary Interpretation.* Chicago: University of Chicago Press, 180-199.

Minnis, A.J., and A.B. Scott. 1988. *Medieval Literary Theory and Criticism c. 1100-c.1375: The Commentary Tradition.* Oxford: Clarendon.

Murray, K.M. Elisabeth. 1979. *Caught in the Web of Words: James Murray and the Oxford English Dictionary.* Oxford: Oxford University Press.

38

Schleicher, August. 1863. *Die Darwinische theorie und die Sprachwissenschaft.* Weimar: Bohlan.

Schwartz, Alexander. 1983. "The Revival of Philology." *Michigan Germanic Studies* 9, 45-62.

Zitselsberger, Otto. 1981. "The Filiation of the Manuscripts of *Konrads saga keisarasonar.*" *Amsterdamer Beitrage zur Älteren Germanistik* 66, 145-176.

Zumthor, Paul. 1972. *Essai de Poetique Médiévale.* Paris: Seuil.

CHAPTER TWO

THE MEDIEVAL BALLADS: TEXTUAL PROBLEMS OF POPULAR LITERATURE

Karin Boglund-Logopoulos

TEXTUALITY OF THE MEDIEVAL BALLAD

The ballads of medieval England pose very particular problems of textuality, problems that could perhaps be summed up by the question, is there such a thing as a medieval ballad text at all? Thus they can offer us a kind of workshop for the study of medieval textuality, especially for the problems we encounter in trying to locate and define any part of what, for lack of a better term, we might call the "popular" literature of the Middle Ages. It is notoriously difficult to define popular literature in any period, but for the Middle Ages I would suggest that a negative definition is the most operational one: popular literature can be considered to be literature composed for a non-courtly, non-clerical audience.[1]

Several aspects of this definition require clarifying discussion. The first concerns the use of the audience, rather than the author's social background, as criterion. The reasons for this are theoretical as well as practical. On the one hand, the greater part of medieval popular literature is utterly anonymous; even in the case of courtly or clerical texts where we know the name of the author, we rarely have much information about him/her. But in addition, authors adopt the styles and conventions that their public approves of, independently of their own origins. In the area of popular literature, then, an approach oriented toward reception theory is likely to be more productive.

A second issue for discussion concerns the concept of non-clerical literature. This at first sight seems fairly straightforward: obviously anything written in Latin would automatically be excluded from most any definition of medieval popular literature. However, there is an enormous body of material produced under the auspices of the church, in the vernacular, specifically for popular consumption: sermons, devotional literature, religious lyrics and carols, to some extent the whole of medieval drama.

We have every indication that the intended audience for this material—evidently not limited to the court or the clergy—was genuinely pious and devoted and found it very much to their taste, so we can scarcely consider it all as foisted upon them by authoritarian methods, though there is obviously an element of indoctrination in the teaching activities of the medieval church. Religious material in a popular context is thus a category which has to be handled rather carefully. This is particularly true in the case of the carols; it is much less so in the case of the ballads, for reasons which I believe will become clear if we consider briefly the nature of the ballad as a genre.

Though the earliest texts of the kind of songs that we today call *ballads* date from the late Middle Ages, the name would not have been applied to them at that time. *Ballade* was the term used for a courtly verse form with strict metrical and stanzaic rules, imported from France. Texts that look like modern ballads are usually described in the Middle Ages as 'songs' 'ditties', 'rimes' or 'talkings'. But the same terms may also be applied to texts which we would today consider a quite different genre, notably the carol and the romance. It thus becomes extremely difficult to distinguish, in the very scanty written sources that mention popular songs at all, what kind of popular song is being described at any particular time, and hence how we should imagine our medieval 'ballad' texts being performed.

The modern distinction between ballad and carol was first attempted systematically by Greene in 1935, and his criteria are still widely accepted by scholars. Greene defines the carol as a dance song, though after ca. 1500 its connection with the dance is apparently weakened. Ballads may also occasionally have been danced (the Scandinavian ballad is usually danced in the Middle Ages, and Scandinavian influence is documented for the ballads of northeastern England and Scotland), but it was not generally a dance song in England [Metzner: 338-340; Buchan (b): 104]. Nevertheless the primary distinction between the two genres for Greene is formal. The carol consists of regular stanzas of varying length, typically rhyming a/a/a/b, and always with a burden sung at the beginning of the carol and after each stanza, whereas the ballad, if it has a burden at all, will have it intercalated between the narrative lines of the stanza. The ballad stanza itself is either in long couplets or (this is considered a later form) in four short lines rhyming a/b/c/b. Later scholars, though disagreeing about particular borderline cases, have generally accepted Greene's definitions: Müller follows Greene, and Fowler (Fowler: 20–42) on the whole accepts Greene's views with the qualification that he does not see any evidence for the existence of the ballad as a clearly defined form before the mid-fifteenth century; before that he believes that we can only speak generally of 'folksong'. Thus, although there are borderline cases among the earliest texts, Greene's formal criteria are remarkably effective in sorting out these two types of songs. To try to distinguish the two on the basis of subject matter is rather more confusing. It is true that the ballad is a narrative song, but the carol may also tell a story at times.

However, a criterion that was probably insignificant in the Middle Ages but which became curcial in the modern definition of the ballad and in its later development, is the fact of the transmission of ballad texts in an oral literary tradition. This method of transmission is essential to the modern concept of the ballad, both because oral transmission influences the poetic structure of the ballad texts, and because in later centuries it is primarily its life in oral tradition which marks the ballad as literature of the 'people' and as distinct from the written genres of upper-class culture. The interaction between written and oral literary traditions in the Middle Ages is a very thorny problem, but as Greene points out, the medieval carol, as it has come down to us, is in significant respects dependent on written transmission. This is connected, he observes, with the use of the carol by the Fransiscan friars in their efforts at religious education: the extensive rewriting of popular carols to give them a didactic or devotional content is a process which removes the texts from a purely popular context and creates a reliance on written rather than oral transmission. There are several carols recorded by Greene, and several songs included in other collections, which are not religious in nature. These analogies can often be found in more recent folksongs. But the majority of the medieval carols as we have them were written *for* the people and are not folksongs in the usual sense of the word.

The ballad, however, seems not to have lent itself to adaptation for clerical purposes, probably because of its narrative character: if one changes the lyrics of a carol but keeps the same melody and burden it may still be felt to be in some sense the same song; if one changes the story of a ballad it simply is not the same ballad. We are thus fairly safe in considering the ballad a non-clerical genre, not of course entirely independent of writing, but not dependent exclusively upon literacy and the written word for its preservation and performance.[2] It is more difficult to determine to what extent it is also non-courtly. Actually, the high courtly style, with its elaborate literary conventions, strong French influence, chivalric values and selfconscious references to tradition, is quite foreign to the ballad texts, as it is to most of Middle English literature outside the very limited circle of the royal court and the high nobility. But some of the earliest ballad texts show a certain degree of courtly influence; the *Gest of Robyn Hode*, for example, adopts certain thematic and stylistic conventions from courtly literature (as has been pointed out by Fowler: 72–78, and most emphatically recently by Holt: 125–126), and *The Battle of Otterburn* has a highly chivalric value structure.

No scholar would seriously argue that the medieval English or Scottish ballads are primarily an aristocratic genre. But in trying to determine the audience for the medieval ballads, we encounter some of the same problems that are involved in defining the audience of the Middle English metrical romances: who listened to them? who performed them, how, and in what circumstances? who wrote them down, and why? The late medieval ballad and the metrical romances are in fact closely related from this point of view. Both are forms of narrative poetry, and both apparently appealed to a similar audience. Ballad and romance texts are found together in the same manuscripts (Garbáty: 287); indeed the Percy folio itself includes both genres indiscriminately.

From this evidence Fowler has argued that the ballad genre as a whole is derived from the romance through the agency of the medieval minstrels. The minstrels, according to Fowler, in the later Middle Ages had to make a living from a more popular audience (he seems to see it primarily as the provincial gentry) when the tastes of the high aristocracy turned to new kinds of entertainment; they then rewrote the old chivalric stories of the romances in a style that gradually led to the ballad. The theory has not won acceptance from all ballad scholars (cf. Müller: 84), perhaps because Fowler's distinction between professional minstrel and amateur ballad singer seems at once too absolute and too dependent on a parallel distinction between "artful" individual creation and "popular" collective repetition (see, e.g., Fowler: 87). Of course ballads and romances might be performed by minstrels, but not everyone who recited ballads and romances need have been a professional. Holt cites a 1469 royal document to the effect that "rough peasants and craftsmen...occupied in various arts and activities on week-days...on feast-days they travel from place to place, and take all the profits on which our aforesaid minstrels...who are learned and instructed on this art and occupation, and versed in no other work, occupation, or mystery, ought to live" (Holt: 128-137). Sloth in *Piers Plowman* knows "rimes of Robin Hood" and is certainly not a professional minstrel, and there is no indication that the shepherds in the *Complaynte of Scotland* are anything but amateurs.[3] It is more likely that ballads and romances alike were performed by both professionals and amateurs for an audience including the households of the provincial gentry, town markets on parish feast-days, and indeed any small gathering that might want entertainment.

The romances are, on the whole, longer texts and make more use of courtly and chivalric elements in plot structure, context and characterization. This would, on the face of it, make them on the whole more dependent on written transmission and professional performance, and more 'gentrified' in their appeal. Some of the earliest ballad texts, notably the *Gest of Robyn Hode*, *Robin Hood and the Monk*, and *Robin Hood and the Potter*, are also rather too long and elaborate to be products of exclusively oral transmission. But there is good evidence that there were sung ballads in circulation during the fifteenth century: a "song of robyn hode" is mentioned as early as 1410 (Chambers: 130; other examples in Fowler: 66–70). More importantly, works that did not make their way into the repertory of sung ballads did not survive in popular tradition. Some time during the fifteenth and sixteenth centuries there was a change in popular literary fashion: the metrical romance effectively died out as a genre. Some of its stories survived, but were made over into ballad form.

Thus the character of the ballad as a primarily oral form seems to apply to the genre from its formation. A correlate of this is that if we find that a medieval text that looks like a ballad is recognizably related to a ballad culled from later oral tradition, we have good reason to suppose that something like the medieval text was in oral circulation at the time when it was recorded in writing. And if the medieval ballad is primarily an oral genre, then we are justified in considering it popular. Metzner (Metzner: 334) points out that the very rarity of early written ballad texts shows that from its inception the genre was *not* considered interesting by the more cultured social strata, though in the provincial society of medieval England and Scotland members of the gentry would of course have listened to ballads (just as they watched mystery plays), and some of them apparently liked certain pieces well enough to record them in a commonplace book.[4] Certainly when we find ballads mentioned in other medieval sources, as we saw above, they are considered as proper to a thoroughly popular milieu.

The negative correlate of this is that medieval ballads rarely get written down at all, and when they do—especially in the earliest texts—they are likely to have been altered in the process. It is not very helpful to know that people sang ballads in the Middle Ages if we have no way of telling what they sounded like. Although ballad scholars generally agree that the English and Scottish ballads have their origin in the late Middle Ages, very few of the texts in Child's enormous collection can actually be traced back with any certainty before ca. 1600.

In selecting a corpus of medieval ballad texts for analysis, I used the following criteria:

a. The text must be a narrative, stanzaic composition, *prima facie* meant to be sung.[5]

b. It must be attested in oral tradition during the Middle Ages or later.

c. A written text recognizably related to the later oral version must have been preserved from before 1600.

The Corpus:

1. *Judas* (Child 23). From MS B14.39, Library of Trinity College, Cambridge; thirteenth century.
2. *The Wee Wee Man* (Child 38). From MS Cotton Julius A.V, British Library; fourteenth century.
3. *Riddles Wisely Expounded* (Child 1). From Rawlinson MS D.328, Bodleian; before 1445.

4. *Thomas Rymer* (Child 37). From the Thornton MS, leaf 149; mid-fifteenth century.

5. *Saint Stephen and Herod* (Child 22). From MS Sloane 2593, British Library; before 1450.

6. *Robyn and Gandeleyn* (Child 115). From MS Sloane 2593, British Library; before 1450.

7. *Robin Hood and the Monk* (Child 119). From MS F.f.5. 28, Library of the University of Cambridge, mid-fifteenth century.

8. *A Gest of Robyn Hode* (Child 117). Printed by Wynkyn de Worde; ca. 1500.

9. *Robin Hood and the Potter* (Child 121). From MS E.e.4.35, Library of the University of Cambridge; ca. 1500.

10. *Crow and Pie* (Child 111). From MS Rawlinson C.813, Bodleian; ca. 1500 or later.

11. *King Edward the Fourth and a Tanner of Tamworth* (Child 273). From MS E.e.iv.35.1., Library of the University of Cambridge; ca. 1500.

12. *The Battle of Otterburn* (Child 161). From MS. Cotton Cleopatra Civ, British Library; mid-sixteenth century; text on linguistic grounds dated by Arngart ca. 1450-1475.

13. *The Hunting of the Cheviot* (Chile 162). From MS Ashmole 48, Bodleian; 1550 or later; text on linguistic grounds dated by Arngart end of the fifteenth century.

14. *Adam Bell, Clim of the Clough, and William of Cloudesley.* (Child 116). Broadside ballad printed 1557-1558 (Stationers' Registry entry).

15. *Sir Andrew Barton* (Child 167). From a MS in York Minster Library; sixteenth century.

16. *King John and the Bishop* (Child 45). From MS 255, Corpus Christi College, Oxford; 1550-1570.

17. *Captain Car* (Child 178). From MS Cotton Vespasian A.xxv, British Library; late sixteenth century.

18. *Flodden Field* (Child 168). Included in Thomas Deloney's *Jack of Newbury*, first published 1597 (the version in MS Harleian 293, second half of the sixteenth century, is a different poem).

19. *The Fair Flower of Northumberland* (Child 9). Included in Thomas Deloney's *Jack of Newbury*, first published 1597.

The corpus thus consists of a total of nineteen texts, of which fifteen can be dated to the mid-sixteenth century or earlier, and the remaining four to before 1600.

Few of the texts from before 1560 are absolutely and indisputably considered ballads by all scholars. Fowler questions most of them on the grounds that they may not have been sung but recited, and should therefore be considered transitional forms between ballad and folksong or ballad and romance. Other scholars have refused to admit the religious texts, or have considered some of the texts carols rather than ballads. It seems to me preferable, however, not to exclude texts on any *a priori* grounds if they fit the criteria established above. If some of these texts are transitional forms, they have more in common with the ballad than with any other genre. These are also the texts that are included in most discussions of the medieval ballad, whether they are accepted as *bona fide* ballads or not [cf. Hodgart: 70–72, Buchan (b): 103–104, Müller 1983: 99, Dobson and Taylor, and Fowler: 20–95).

The modern ballad has a strongly regional character, and there is every reason to suppose that the medieval ballad had one as well. It is, however, impossible to attempt to define regional differences on the basis of such a limited corpus. The very fact that continued presence in oral tradition is one of the criteria used in selecting the texts will have biased the corpus in the direction of northern England and Scotland, where the oral tradition of balladry was strongest in more recent times.[6]

THE SEMANTIC UNIVERSE OF THE BALLADS

The medieval ballads thus form a very small, one might almost say insignificant, part of the body of ballad texts collected in later centuries, and they have not generally been the concern of ballad scholarship. Ballad scholars have traditionally concentrated on the historical development of the genre, taxonomies of national ballad traditions, comparisons of versions and variants, establishment of a regional corpus, or the study of certain techniques of narrative structuring characteristic of oral tradition [cf. Müller and, for a more formal approach, Buchan (a)]. The specifically medieval ballads have rarely been studied from the point of view of their literary characteristics at all; the only exceptions to date are Fowler's (1978) seminal book and a few more analytical studies of individual ballads. Interest has been directed almost exclusively to the ballad texts as evidence for historical developments, and especially to the Robin Hood ballads (cf. Hilton, Keen, Benecke, Holt, Dobson and Taylor). But the medieval ballads, with their rather unique position as evidence of an oral, popular literary life and their particular problems of textuality present a very special interest to medievalists and should not be ignored by them.[7]

This paper proposes to make a small contribution in this direction by analysing the semantic universe of the medieval ballad texts. The method is based on A.J. Greimas' *Sémantique structurale*, especially on the two concepts of *isotopy* and *code*.

Briefly, an *isotopy* is an empirical grouping-together of semantic units (which on the level of analysis here attempted can be taken, in a simplified sense, to be words) that in the analyst's judgment seem to 'belong together'. This group of terms is then reviewed and an attempt is made to discover the principle of its semantic structure: what it is that these units have in common (why we feel that they 'belong together') and how they can be organized. In the process the original grouping may be modified: some terms may in the final analysis fit better elsewhere. When the isotopy has been organized into a structure, it is called a *code*. We may give it a name of our own invention which can conveniently be used as an indication of the semantic area it covers: a code of loyalty, a code of warfare, an erotic code, etc. (I should mention that a code contains both positive terms and their opposites: loyalty vs. treason, war vs. peace, desire vs. repulsion, and so on.)

The codes used in a text make up its semantic universe. The text relates its codes in certain ways, defines its characters (actors) by giving them attributes from these codes, and effects transformations in the structure of its semantic universe through the changing relationships created by the episodes in its narrative.

The actual structuring and relationships of particular codes vary from one ballad to another, but the use of a certain *set* of codes (a certain core semantic universe) seems to be a characteristic that can be used to group ballads together into sub-genres. This is by no means a new discovery. Scholars have long classified ballads on the basis of their subject matter, that is, by a more empirical and approximative use of semantic isotopies. However, these taxonomies generally concern the whole corpus of a national ballad tradition taken ahistorically [cf. Metzner: 348–352, Buchan (b): 99–100] and are often applied to the medieval texts in a somewhat *a priori* fashion. A taxonomy based on the internal characteristics of the medieval ballad texts themselves would raise interesting issues of comparison with the groupings of later ballad texts.[8]

The ballads in our corpus can be grouped, on the basis of shared sets of semantic codes, into six major groups: historical ballads, outlaw ballads, humourous ballads, spell ballads, romantic ballads, and religious ballads.

THE HISTORICAL BALLADS

What makes a ballad seem 'historical' is the strong stylistic presence of a register of *realism*, which upon closer examination is found to consist of three main codes: frequent use of real or realistic *names*, an elaborate set of *personal names* and titles, and careful indications of the *time* when particular events are said to have taken place. No actual historical truth is implied by the use of this register, though of course, historical truth is not excluded either; the realistic register is simply a stylistic device. Ballads in other groups use the realistic register to a lesser extent and in a more simplified form.

In addition to their stylistic realism, all the historical ballads in the corpus use what we might call a code of *warfare* (references to battles, armies, weapons, death). The burial of the dead and the laments of widows and orphans seem to be an established part of the warfare code. Likewise, all use a code of *strength*, usually including the notion of courage (moral strength) and often that of skill with weapons.

Frequent, but not universal, is the use of a *technical* code, such as hunting or sailing. Chivalry, in the sense of courtly behaviour, is rather rare (the presence of a strong courtly code is what distinguishes *The Battle of Otterburn* from *The Hunting of the Cheviot*), but a code of *loyalty* (as opposed to treason) is frequently used. A nationalistic *social* code (Englishmen vs. Scotsmen) is usual but of varying importance; *nobility* of birth appears but without special emphasis, and a *sexual* code (man vs. woman) occurs once, in *Captain Car*.

Boasts or vows and their performance are fairly common as a device of plot structure (they serve to create an obligation on the part of the hero or villain when no motivation is readily available). A code of religious *devotion* is optional and can be used to provide ethical sanction for one set of characters rather than another, though ethical value is usually attached directly to the codes of strength/courage and loyalty.

The ballads from our corpus that can be grouped together as historical ballads on the basis of this shared set of codes are *The Battle of Otterburn*, *The Hunting of the Cheviot*, *Sir Andrew Barton*, *Captain Car*, and *Flodden Field*. The first two exist in MSS of the mid-sixteenth century but can be dated on linguistic evidence to the latter half of the fifteenth century (Arngart); the remaining three are all sixteenth-century texts. All are well attested in later ballad tradition. This group corresponds to the group Buchan [Buchan (b):100] refers to in the general corpus of British balladry as Historical and Semi-Historical Ballads. The historical ballad is thus a strong and well-established category, both in the medieval corpus and in later ballad tradition.

THE OUTLAW BALLADS

If we compare the semantic universe of the historical ballads with that of the outlaw ballads in our corpus, certain similarities and differences are immediately apparent. The *realistic* register, to begin with, is weaker than in the historical ballads: indications of time, place and person are more rudimentary, though still specific. The outlaw ballads also use a weakened form of the code of *warfare* or rather of smaller confrontations and fights, in which there is included a fairly elaborate machinery of prisons, gates, walls, gallows, and so on. *Strength*, courage and skill in arms figure as prominently as in the historical ballads.

The outlaw ballads thus have a nexus of codes in common with the historical ballads, though they differ in the emphasis and relative elaboration they give each code. This is also true in the case of the code of *loyalty*, which is the most significant ethical code in the outlaw ballads: it appears in all the texts and has a very central role to play both in plot structure and in the moral stance of the singer vis-à-vis his material. The outlaw ballads consistently use only one technical code, that of *archery*, and this is present as a game or contest as often as it appears as a weapon.

Unique to the outlaw ballads is a *social* code that divides the world into outlaws vs. officials. Other people are placed with the one or the other category on rather variable grounds. Only the *Gest of Robyn Hode* makes a deliberate and systematic extension of these categories to poor vs. rich. Most texts consider bishops, abbots and monks as classifiable with the officials (sheriff, justice, etc.), and usually the criterion for being considered a member of "the good guys" is strength and courage (being a 'Ffelowe') rather than birth, position or even income. It should however be said that the 'Ffelawes' tend to be yeomen. The outlaw ballads are definitely not interested in starting a popular revolution: there is no indication of any political code (as indeed Child pointed out) in these ballads and it is not even clear whether the people in general sympathize with the outlaws all the time.

What they *are* interested in, however, is living a life of plenty. *Wealth* as such is often a fairly important code in the outlaw ballads (ranging from a meal and suit of clothes to four hundred pounds in gold). It enters into a curious complex of codes that we might call the *greenwood* register: this includes the status of outlaw; the activity of shooting the king's deer, robbing incautious travelers and feasting on the abundant proceeds from this business; often the archery contest; sometimes references to life in the woods, specific landmarks (such as the trysting-tree), or general atmosphere (green leaves, birdsong). It is a semantic complex curiously similar to the concept of courtliness in the courtly romances, from which in fact it has borrowed some features such as feasting, abundance, and merriment; it is present in all the outlaw ballads to some extent, but very much elaborated in the *Gest of Robyn Hode*, which (as we already mentioned) also makes prominent use of the code of *courtliness* (otherwise rare in the outlaw ballads—indeed in any of the ballads in the corpus).

A final code that is nearly universal in the outlaw ballads, though not confined only to this group, is what we might call the code of *trickery*. The use of disguise in some form is essential to the plot of almost all the outlaw ballads. This code is not to be confused with the code of loyalty vs. treachery, which is an ethical issue and has nothing to do with trickery; tricks are legitimate tactics in the outlaw ballads.

Optional in the outlaw ballads as in the historical ballads is the use of *boasts* or vows to structure the plot; the occasional use of a *sexual* code; and a code of religious *devotion*. Robin Hood's devotion to the Virgin Mary, in addition to providing him with moral sanction, serves various purposes in plot structure: it may be the reason for breaking an injunction (going to Nottingham to hear Mass), it may be a form of loyalty (helping a poor knight because he invokes the Virgin as security), or occasionally it may justify supernatural assistance (in being rescued from prison).

The texts in our corpus which share these codes and which thus can be considered outlaw ballads are *Robin Hood and the Monk, A Gest of Robyn Hode, Robin Hood and the Potter*, and *Adam Bell, Clem of the Clough and William of Cloudesley*. The texts date from ca. 1450–1550, and although these particular texts are not found in oral tradition at a later date, the matter of Robin Hood is most thoroughly established as being the subject of songs, plays, dances and popular entertainments in the fourteenth, fifteenth and sixteenth centuries.[10] The outlaw ballads as a group are thus also a strong and well-established category of the corpus. They apparently correspond to what ballad scholars have called Ballads of Yeoman Minstrelsy in the whole corpus of British balladry [Buchan (b):100].

With the outlaw ballads we also group the text of *Robyn and Gandeleyn*. This text shows all the essential codes of the outlaw ballad, although some of them are very lightly represented. The only code not found is that of trickery. Strength, courage and skill in arms is certainly used; loyalty vs. treachery is explicitly included; the archery contest is used ironically in the dialogue between Gandeleyn and Wrennock; the greenwood register appears in the early stanzas and in the refrain; the illegal hunting of the king's deer and the opposition to some sort of owner or warden has to be assumed in order to make sense of Wrennock's shooting of Robyn. Its semantic universe would clearly classify this ballad as an outlaw ballad.

THE HUMOROUS BALLADS

This is another group of texts in which *trickery* is also essential to the plot (whether deliberate or inadvertent, as in the Tanner of Tamworth who fails to recognize the king). The *realistic* register is present but no very strongly, and a fairly strong code of *wealth* is important; a *social* code, though somewhat rudimentary, opposes the hero and his helpers to kings, lords and nobles. Aside from these, the other codes used seem to depend on the particular story. *King John and the Bishop* uses the riddle dialogue to structure the plot. *The Tanner of Tamworth* makes humorous and ironic use of the code of courtliness, as the Tanner is consistently churlish in reply to the king's polite manners.

The humorous ballads thus have a core of codes in common with the outlaw ballads, and indeed it seems that storytellers have felt the similarity: in other versions of the story of the Tanner of Tamworth (but not in ballads; see Child), the tale is expanded to include the outlaw element of illegal hunting, and the incognito monarch is treated to a feast of his own venison.

The texts in this category are *King Edward the Fourth and a Tanner of Tamworth* and *King John and the Bishop*. Both are sixteenth-century texts. There are not as many texts in this category, but I think it must still be considered a well-established group, perhaps proportionally better represented in the medieval corpus than in later balladry; in Buchan's taxonomy, the Comic Ballads are a sub-genre.

THE SPELL BALLADS

Essential to the spell ballads is a *cosmological* code spatially relating the world of men to the world of supernatural beings, usually fairies but often the devil as well (his counterpart, God, is included rather by implication, if at all). The most elaborate cosmology is found in *Thomas Rymer* (or *Thomas of Erceldoune* as the fifteenth-century text is titled), where the queen of fairies meets Thomas under the Eldone tree and leads him down through Eldone Hill and across a water until they come to an orchard; there she points out to him four roads, one over a mountain to heaven, one across a rise to paradise, one under a plain to purgatory and one down through a dell to hell. The site of her husband's castle is on a hill close to this point, apparently in the direction of hell. This is a very thorough spatial scheme, but its most important points, which are shared by other spell ballads, are that fairies live underneath the earth, that there are certain places where one can enter their realm, that they have a special relationship to certain natural features or plants (hills, trees, flowers, bushes), and that they are in some sense in league with the devil. Thus a code of human vs. non-human is closely related to this cosmology. A code of *magical power* is also important: the fairies place humans under an enchantment or spell which must be broken by a particular ritual exorcism.

The relationship between human beings and fairies in our corpus is almost invariably *erotic*. The erotic relationship may in itself constitute the violation that places the human man or woman in the fairy's power, or it can be the reason for escaping. A *sexual* code (man vs. woman) usually coincides with the human vs. non-human distinction and the lover vs. mistress of the erotic code. Often there is a code of true vs. false *appearances* or strange transformations of appearance. The *realistic* register varies tremendously, from fairly strong in *Thomas of Erceldoune* to virtually nonexistent in *The Wee Wee Man*. The code of *nature* to some extent takes the place of the realistic register, since one inevitably meets fairies out of doors, often by picking flowers or while lying under a tree. Other codes are optional. *Courtliness* may appear, as it does in *Thomas of Erceldoune* . *Minstrelsy*, music, singing and dancing seem to be favorite activities of fairies.

Characteristic of the plot structure, in addition to the violation of an injunction (such as not speaking to the fairy or not taking anything he/she proffers), seems to be that the hero or heroine often has some quality that acts as a talisman, or that makes a fairy helper like and protect him or her, such as being a *loyal* lover, being *wise* enough to answer all the devil's riddles.

Evidently we are here in a semantic universe very different from that of the historical ballads or outlaw ballads. The essential codes of the two groups are quite distinct, and the only codes they have in common are the weak or optional ones used for stylistic elaboration (e.g., courtliness) or those that distinguish an individual story. The realistic codes both differ in emphasis and are differently related to the other codes. Entirely different articulations are selected for the social codes: English vs. Scots or outlaws vs. officials in one case, human vs. non-human in the other. What may be an incidental plot variation in the historical and outlaw ballads, such as the role of women in the plot, is crucial to the spell ballads where the relationship between two worlds is articulated through the erotic relationship of a man and a woman (or rather a male and a female, whether human or not).

The ballads in our corpus that share this semantic structure are *The Wee Wee Man*, *Riddles Wisely Expounded*, and *Thomas Rymer*. None of them is entirely without textual problems. *The Wee Wee Man*, earliest of the group and one of the earliest of all the texts in the corpus, is evidently a spell story but seems to lack an ending. In the fourteenth-century manuscript which has the text I use here, the reason for this is evidently that the song is used to introduce a string of prophecies, and the text never gets back to the beginning of the frame story again. Later versions recovered from oral tradition show the same non-determined ending: in the last two lines of the last stanza, the wee wee man simply vanishes away and the speaker is presumably free to go home. The fourteenth-century text is not, as it stands, a ballad, and Child prints it as an appendix rather than as an earlier version of the song. It has enough verbal parallels with the later texts, however, that we must postulate some relationship. The early text looks to me like a rather poorly padded version of the later ballad, but it could conceivably also have been taken up into popular song from a written original; if so, it was much improved in the process. This is also the only spell ballad where the sex of the human party (the speaker of the text) is left unclear; later versions sometimes remedy this oversight and make the speaker a lady.

The second text that I have classified as a spell ballad is the early fifteenth-century riddle sequence entitled *Inter Diabolus et Virgo*, which Child prints as an appendix to *Riddles Wisely Expounded*. The sequence bears a close resemblance to the riddle song *I Have a Yong Suster* in MS Sloane 2593 (dated to before 1450). We cannot know if *Inter Diabolus et Virgo* was sung as the later ballad was, but the riddle sequence has been integrated into a narrative framework, and that framework has most of the essential features of a spell ballad. The devil appears to a maid and threatens to make her his lemman if she cannot answer his riddles; the girl prays to Jesus who evidently comes to her aid, for she then answers all of them. In later versions the last riddle is often "what is worse than woman was?" and she answers that the Devil is worse, whereupon the fiend is exorcised and vanishes in a puff of smoke. As in *King John and the Bishop*, the popular riddle song has been adapted to a ballad framework, this time with the spell ballad's complex of codes: hence the presence of the erotic element in the devil's threat. The fact that it has thus become in a certain sense a religious text perhaps explains its early written appearance.

The text of *Thomas of Erceldoune* is also not a popular text. It is used to introduce a lengthy prophetic text, and it makes marked use of the descriptive techniques of the courtly style. But the ballad of *Thomas Rymer* recovered later from oral recitation shows close verbal parallels with the earlier text, and unless we want to assume that the singer, Mrs. Brown of Falkland, deliberately refurbished a book of fifteenth-century prophecies, by far the most sensible explanation of its history is that a version close to the fifteenth-century text was in circulation among singers between the time of the composition of *Thomas of Erceldoune* and the mid-eighteenth century when Mrs. Brown learned her ballad repertoire.

Thus, each of the early spell ballads in our corpus is in some sense problematic, mostly in that the texts we have seem to be adaptations of ballad texts rather than ballads themselves. It would seem that spell ballads are fairly well established as a group in the medieval corpus, but not as strongly as the other groups we have examined, and certainly not as strongly as the group of magical and marvelous ballads in the British ballad corpus as a whole. I would suggest that this has to do with problems in the transmission of the earliest texts, a point to which I will return below.

THE ROMANTIC BALLADS

Some elements from the semantic universe of the spell ballads occur in the romantic ballads as well. The romantic and tragic ballads form an important part of later ballad tradition; in the Middle Ages, however, this group is poorly attested and has generally weak textual links to the period before 1600. The one undisputedly early sixteenth-century text, *Crow and Pie*, has a closer relationship to some of the carols than to ballads, handles its topic comically throughout, and never recurs in later oral tradition in this form (though there are similar pieces). One other text, *The Fair Flower of Northumberland*, is included by Thomas Deloney in *Jack of Newbury* in 1597. This is not a very satisfactory state of affairs, and it may well be that the whole sub-genre of romantic ballads is a development of the seventeenth century, only embryonically present in our period.

As they stand, these texts are the result of an articulation of the *erotic* and *sexual* codes with a *social* code in which the girl and/or her family vs. the lover is the essential element (sometimes reinforced by additional oppositions such as noble vs. common, rich vs. poor, English vs. Scots), and with a code of *loyalty* vs. treachery (here, the issue is being a loyal or a deceitful lover). The *realistic* register is very weak, with very poor indications of time, place or characterization.

Optionally, women characters may be distinguished by a code of *beauty* vs. ugliness; men characters usually by *courtliness* and manners. The use of false *appearances* is possible, but the code of *violoence* (murder, suicide, revenge) which is often necessary for the resolution of later Romantic and Tragic Ballads is entirely missing from the medieval texts. In fact the medieval ballads have a curious sort of happy ending. The girl is tricked by a false lover, but in one case sends him packing with a curse, having taken her heart back (*Crow and Pie*); in the other she returns home to her parents having learned not to trust a Scotsman. The tragic ending, that of the family of one or the other party intervening disastrously and the girl and/or the lover dying or killing themselves, seems to be a later development altogether.

THE RELIGIOUS BALLADS

One of the problems with the religious ballads is that they do not form a coherent group. The oldest, *Judas*, exists only in one thirteenth-century text and has no continuity in oral tradition, though the story exists as a folktale. The second, *Saint Stephen and Herod*, also exists only in one mid-fifteenth century manuscript and has no continuity in English oral tradition but appears as a Christmas carol in Scandinavia. Some scholars consider the *Corpus Christi Carol* (Balliol College, Oxford MA 354,

early sixteenth century) as a religious ballad, although its narrative
content is really less than minimal.

To try to define what these texts have in common, except a
narrative sequence and a set of characters drawn from Christian
myth and legend, is not an easy task. One of the stories is told,
interestingly enough, from the villain's point of view, which makes
the central character into a kind of tragic hero. Judas is the victim
of a kind of *failed recognition*, mistaking an actual adversary
(Pilate) for a potential helper. Perhaps one could argue that
recognition (successful in this case) is crucial to the story of St.
Stephen as well, as he succeeds in recognizing the newborn Christ
which Herod fails to do.

In both texts, a crucial code is that of *loyalty* to one's
master. Judas evidently fails in loyalty when he allows himself to
be tricked by his sister; Stephen declares that he is forsaking
Herod for a new master, the "chyld in Bedlam born".

We could perhaps argue that a code which these texts also
share is one which opposes different kinds of *value* : the value of
one's Lord vs. the thirty pieces of silver for the food Judas was
sent to buy; meat, drink, clothing and fee vs. the salvation of one's
soul in the case of St. Stephen.

But there is no avoiding the conclusion that what really
groups these texts together is their common link with the ethical
system, the myths and legends, of the Christian religion. This
semantic universe also provides their 'realistic' register of time,
place and persons, a set of references which in the Middle Ages
would have been considered real enough, but not as close to the
everyday world as the references of the historical or outlaw
ballads. Religious ballads exist as a sub-genre, though with
comparatively few recorded texts, both in the medieval corpus
and in modern taxonomies.

OVERLAPPING AND INTERSECTING SEMANTIC UNIVERSES

Comparing the semantic structures of the six groups of
ballads we have divided our corpus into, we already noticed that
some of them can be fairly closely related to each other. We saw
that the humourous ballads draw on some of the codes of the

outlaw ballads, and that there is some overlapping between the spell ballads and the romantic ballads. It is also evident that the historical ballads share a whole nexus of codes with the outlaw ballads. The six groups of texts might thus be related as follows:

The historical ballads and the outlaw ballads share, though with differing emphasis, codes of warfare and strength/courage, the use of a technical code, the realistic register, and often a code of loyalty; they are most clearly distinguished by differing social codes and by the outlaw ballad's use of trickery and of the greenwood register. The outlaw ballads share with the humourous ballads the code of trickery and often of wealth, and partly the same social code (see diagram 1).

The core of the similarity between the spell ballads and the romantic ballads lies in the erotic and sexual codes and in the frequent use of true vs. false appearances. They are distinguished rather sharply by the essential role of the code of loyalty vs. treachery in the romantic ballads and by their very different social codes. The spell ballads also make use of a much richer semantic universe than the romantic ballads, with the cosmological and the magical codes and the code of nature.

The religious ballads are so strongly marked by their relation to the semantic universe of the Christian religion that it is difficult to group them with any of the other ballad texts. Their implied cosmology would relate them to the spell ballads, but they make little actual use of cosmological organization (the spell ballads are much more obviously supernatural than the religious ballads in our corpus). The significance of loyalty to a master in the religious ballads could group them with the outlaw ballads or with the romantic ballads; the use of the opposition of loyalty to a master vs. loyalty to your kinswomen in *Judas* would in fact relate it very closely to the romantic ballads, even more so if Dronke is correct in interpreting Judas' 'sister' as his mistress, which would reinforce the latent erotic code implied when she 'seduces' Judas into falling asleep with his head in her lap. The element of failed recognition or false appearances is also common to the religious ballads and the outlaw and romantic ballads, and since the role of this element is generally not the comic one of trickery but the tragic one of deceit or treachery, it would relate them most closely to the romantic ballads. The two solitary religious ballads in our corpus have too few elements in common, beyond their dependence on the Christian semantic universe, to allow us to relate them as a

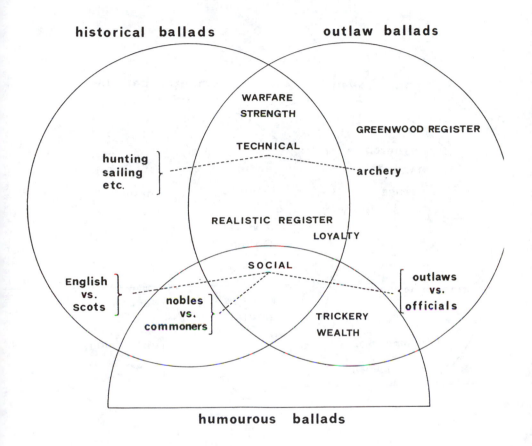

Diagram 1.   Semantic universe of the historical, outlaw and humorous ballads.

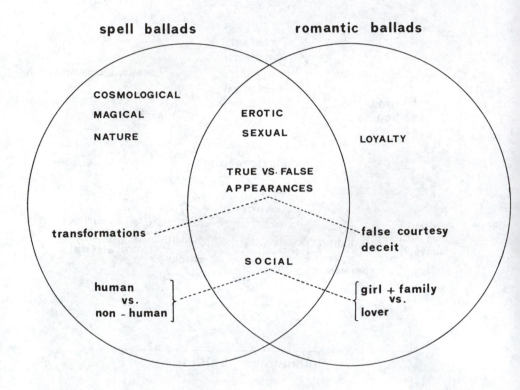

Diagram 2. Semantic universe of the spell ballads and romantic ballads.

group to any other group of ballad texts. But *Judas* taken alone should perhaps be considered the first of the English romantic and tragic ballads to have been preserved in writing, though it is of course an atypical composition (cf. also Dronke: 61–63, Stouck, Müller: 173).

THE MEDIEVAL BALLAD TEXTS AND LATER BALLADRY: PROBLEMS OF TEXTUALITY

As we saw, a taxonomy of medieval ballad texts based on their internal semantic structures shows both similarities and differences with the customary modern classification of British ballads. Of the three major and five minor sub-genres that Buchan mentions [Buchan (b): 100], all three major and three, maybe four of the minor sub-genres are represented in the medieval corpus. The late middle ages show (to use Buchan's terminology) well-established historical ballads and fairly well-established magical ballads, although few romantic ballads. Comic ballads and ballads of yeoman minstrelsy are rather more than minor sub-genres since they have a stronger position in the medieval corpus than in later tradition, and some prototype of the religious ballads seems to exist as well. There are in the medieval corpus two riddle ballads, but they seem to fit better together with other sub-genres than as a separate group. Only the so-called ballads of late medieval minstrelsy are not represented in our analysis, probably because before 1600 texts of this kind, though printed as broadsides, would better be considered metrical romances.

However, the groups of texts in the medieval corpus show considerable differences with their later counterparts. The groups that most resemble later ballad sub-genres are the historical, outlaw, and comic ballads, and it can scarcely be an accident that these three categories are both richest in recorded medieval texts, and are semantically related to each other. The spell ballads are not nearly as well represented in the medieval corpus as one might expect, considering that many magical ballads recorded later are judged on internal evidence to be of medieval origin. But the most striking difference between the medieval corpus and later balladry is certainly the very poor representation of medieval romantic ballads, especially when we recall that the modern category is actually romantic and tragic ballads. Although the conflict between love and family that ends in tragedy is so common as to be almost stereotypical of later balladry and although many famous tragic ballads (*Edward*, *Lord Randall*) are considered by scholars to go back to medieval originals, not a single text of this kind is actually recorded before 1600.

Some texts which would later become romantic ballads appear to have been originally spell ballads (Müller: 44–45), and as spell ballads they may well have existed in the middle ages (a broadside entitled *Tam Lin* is recorded in the Stationers' Registry in 1558). Some romantic ballads are derived from what before 1600 would have been considered romances. But it is striking that the "Familiarismus", the emphasis on conflict and tragedy within the family, that Müller (Müller: 172-178) and others see as so characteristic of later balladry should be completely missing from our corpus. Perhaps with closer philological analysis of individual texts, some later ballads of family tragedy may turn out to be of medieval origin and fill this gap, but if so it is still odd that none of these was ever recorded in the middle ages.

In view of the relationship between the semantic structures of spell ballads and romantic ballads, and the lack of tragic ballads (with the possible exception of *Judas*), which is rather too much of a special case to build an argument upon) in our corpus, it may not be entirely fortuitous that these groups are particularly well represented in the repertoire of Anna Gordon, Mrs. Brown of Falkland, the first ballad singer to provide scholars with something like a full repertoire of the ballads of an individual singer in oral tradition in the late eighteenth century. Two to three hundred years after the period we are concerned with, Buchan [Buchan (a)] considers that these kinds of ballads (in the region of northeast Scotland at least) constituted the main part of a repertoire: Mrs. Brown had learned them from her aunt, who in turn had learned them from nurses and old women. Is it possible that they were part of a *women's* repertoire three centuries earlier?

There are, I think, strong indications that the texts of the first groups, historical, outlaw and humorous ballads, were a women's repertoire. These are the groups of ballads that flourish with the development of the printed broadside, and the production of broadsides was very much in the hands of male writers, printers and peddlers. One would also have to add that the writing down and printing of the spell ballads and romantic ballads was probably also done by a man's hand, which may partly explain why the early texts of the spell ballads often look like adaptations of popular texts for special purposes.

There are some indirect indications that the spell ballads and romantic ballads were felt in the middle ages to be properly the domain of women singers. Thomas Deloney in *Jack of Newbury* (1597) assigns the ballad of *The Fair Flower of Northumberland* to a group of young girls spinning, one singing the verses and the others joining in the burden. In an earlier period, Chaucer ascribes to his Wife of Bath a tale of an erotic relationship between a human knight and a fairy mistress, though here the treatment of the topic is humorous. Even earlier, the *Lais* of Marie de France, an Anglo-Norman poetess, deal with themes closely related to those of the spell ballads and romantic ballads.

On the other hand, the romantic ballads of later centuries seem in many cases to be derived from romances, and romances were the repertoire, first of courtly poets and then of minstrels. Indeed, Fowler argues that many of the early manuscripts in which ballads are found, including the Percy folio, should be considered minstrels' collections of materials: romances, ballads, didactic tales, lyrics and all. It may be possible to connect these fragmentary and contradictory indices by positing a development something like this: the songs and stories that became first the *lais* and later the spell ballads and romantic ballads were originally (in the Celtic areas of Europe, perhaps?) the province of women singers. The courtly romance, however, was developed by male poets and when it used material that was also drawn upon by the *lais*, this material was incorporated into men's repertoires. It may well have continued to be used also by women singers, though the only evidence I know of for this are the indirect indications furnished by Chaucer and Deloney. When the romances fall out of fashion toward the end of the Middle Ages, the material is again taken over by the oral tradition of popular song (if indeed it was ever relinquished entirely) and perhaps appropriated or re-appropriated by women singers.[11]

This hypothesis would explain the problems in the written transmission of both the spell ballads and the romantic ballads in the medieval corpus. The spell ballads are written down only in a form adapted to some other purpose (such as presenting a 'serious' set of prophecies), and the romantic ballads are not yet fully established as a ballad genre but are still half carol or romance. It might also help to explain the absence of the tragic family ballads from the medieval corpus.

A final problem of the textuality of the medieval ballad concerns the relationship of some of the medieval texts to the written literary culture, more especially to courtly literature. The courtly style—the emphasis on elegance in dress and manners, on noble birth and courtly surroundings, the elaborate descriptions that are such a characteristic feature of courtly poetry—is rarely found in the ballads, as we have already remarked. There are three exceptions. In *Thomas of Erceldoune* there is a fairly extensive use of courtly description of dress and manners, a feature which is much simplified in the later ballad as recorded from oral tradition. In *The Battle of Otterburn*, the chivalrous behaviour of the heroes is the ethical issue of the whole poem and a crucial element in the plot. On the other hand, *The Hunting of the Cheviot*, which is a nearly contemporary treatment of the same story, completely ignores the courtly code and relies on plain strength, courage and loyalty to justify its heroes morally.

The third case is *A Gest of Robyn Hode*, an elegant combination of four or five different stories from the Robin Hood material into a longer narrative with a more or less coherent plot: a literary form that the title itself indicates is a *gest*.[12] Robyn Hode and his men are here presented as a kind of ironic or comic equivalent of courtly knights, they welcome guests to the greenwood as if it were a castle, they feast and make merry in a manner reminiscent of Arthur and Gawain, and the poet's description of their feasting shows precisely (though perhaps rather ironically) that emphasis on rich, beautiful material possessions and surroundings that is characteristic of courtly literature. Robyn Hode in fact has set up a kind of rival court in the greenwood, and for all his loyalty to the king he eventually prefers the greenwood to the expensive and boring life of a member of the king's household.

In the case of these three texts, then, we need to be aware that they are out of the ordinary as ballads. As they stand, they are probably not meant for a popular audience at all, certainly not for an exclusively popular one. *Thomas of Erceldoune*, as we saw above, may have adapted popular material for a specific purpose. It is perhaps indicative of this operation that the introductory fit, the story of Thomas and the elf queen which forms the basis for the later ballad, is much better poetry than the prophecies that follow. The *Gest of Roybn Hode* is in many ways a similar case, being both clearly based on material whose popular character is indisputable, and yet clearly a deliberate, written literary creation in itself, but here the author has succeeded in giving his composition a much more coherent plot and more consistent characters, and it has rightly attracted special attention from scholars (Keen, Holt, Benecke).

In the case of the two ballads on the subject of the battle of Otterburn, a comparison of the manuscripts is interesting. The earliest manuscript of the 'courtly' *Battle of Otterburn* (Cotton Cleopatra C.iv) sets out the text neatly in short lines and separate stanzas, leaving wide margins, whereas the manuscript of *The Hunting of the Cheviot* (Ashmole 48) covers the whole page in run-on lines; Skeat comments that it "is a mere scribble, and the spelling very unsatisfactory", and Arngart considers it as transcribed from oral recitation (Arngart:50). It seems that *Cheviot* is a more popular and *Otterburn* a more courtly version of the same story, perhaps an early example of how a ballad can be adapted according to audience and circumstances. Fowler (Fowler: 108–114) considers them as versions of the same ballad, *Cheviot* being the older version, and *Otterburn* based upon it.

Thus, the more we examine each individual text in the medieval corpus, the more we are reminded of the thorniest problem of textuality in the case of the medieval ballads: the simple fact that we have a *text* means that the text is not in its original *context* any more. Even if the text has not been adapted to a different function, it is always true that these texts were meant to be performed, and the whole interplay between performer and audience that would have made up an integral part of the meaning of the songs is necessarily lost to us, the subject of halting reconstruction and guesswork. In this respect, the ballads can stand as a representative example of a whole set of problems of medieval textuality: the set which derives from the presence in almost all of medieval literature, irrespective of its social context, of the interaction between oral performance and written record.

NOTES

1.   Careful and illuminating discussions of the concept of 'popular' literature in the middle ages can be found in Heffernan; especially relevant to our topic are the papers by Robertson and Brewer, and Heffernan's preface.

2.   The conditions of development of the late medieval ballads correspond more closely to what Buchan [Buchan (a)] calls *verbal* transmission: orally communicated in a partly literate society. The term *oral* is reserved by him for non-literate society.

3.   Even the well-read Captain Cox, who performed in a traditional pageant before Queen Elizabeth at Kenilworth Castle in 1575, is a mason by trade, though apparently a minstrel by avocation; see Furnivall: xiv–xv.

4.   Holt (Holt: 109–158) argues for the gentry as the original audience of the Robin Hood ballads. But the evidence he adduces really points to the serving-men of the feudal household rather than to the gentry as such. For discussions of the meaning of the term 'yeoman' in the fifteenth century, see also Hilton, Keen: 128–173, Garbáty, and Dobson and Taylor: 27–36; and cf. Denholm-Young: 25–29.

5.   If a text was included by Child in *The English and Scottish Popular Ballads*, I considered this as prima facie evidence that the text is a ballad.

6.   Buchan [Buchan (b): 105–106] seems to be the only scholar who has even suggested the possibility of considering regional features in discussing medieval English ballads.

7.   I am in effect following Fowler's (Fowler: 3–19) call for a chronological approach to the ballads, as most recent ballad research has done.

8.   Fowler's discussion, though sensitive and insightful, is confusing since he considers most early ballad texts in the context of folksong—Fowler: 20-64.

9. All the medieval ballads irrespective of group frequently include some metalinguistic, phatic framing of the story itself in which the singer addresses his/her audience. Since this is a device virtually universal in medieval literature, the texts of which are almost always adapted for public as well as private reading, I will not discuss it further here.

10. The last few stanzas of the *Gest* allude to the story of the death of Robin Hood, a story which in its full form appears as a ballad both in the Percy folio and in later oral tradition (*Robin Hood's Death*, Child 120).

11. It will be evident that this hypothesis partly conforms to and partly differs from Fowler's account of the development of the ballad from the encounter of late medieval minstrelsy and folksong in the fifteenth century. Mainly, I postulate a continuous substratum of popular song and story rather than a filtering-down of debased artistic compositions by a class of professional minstrels.

12. Unlike Fowler, I do believe that the episodes which are conbined in the *Gest* had a prior independent existence, though I wouldn't venture to say that they were all circulating as full-fledged ballads. Though much of the text of the *Gest* must be the work of the person who composed it in its present form, there is much that is obviously drawn from a common stock with the other, contemporary Robin Hood ballads. Indeed, Benecke's attempts to argue that the *Gest* is the same kind of poem as the outlaw epics of the thirteenth century (*Gesta Herewardi*, *Foulke Fitz Warin*) really tend to point up the *differenences* between these heroes and the Robyn Hode of the *Gest*: the *Gest* cannot be described as a biography of Robin Hood; Robin is not of noble birth and has no inheritance to fight for, does not distinguish himself in knightly combat but in hunting and archery, and cannot convincingly be construed as a representative of the interests of the feudal nobility. It is clear that the author of the *Gest* must have had the outlaw epic (especially perhaps *Gamelyn*) in mind as a model when composing his poem, but it is equally clear that the result is an adaptation to this model of material of rather different character and origin. Cf. also Dobson and Taylor: 32–36, and

68

Keen (the source of the comparison between the outlaw epics and the Robin Hood ballads).

REFERENCES

Arngart, Olof. 1973. *Two English Border Ballads*. Acta Universitatis Lundensis sectio 1. Theologica, Juridica, Humaniora 18. Lund: Gleerups.

Benecke, Ingrid. 1973. *Der gute Outlaw: Studien zu einem literarischen Typus im 13. und 14. Jahrhundert*. Tübingen: Max Niemeyer.

Brewer, Derek. 1985. "The International Medieval Popular Comic Tale in England". In Thomas J. Heffernan, ed., *The Popular Literature of Medieval England*. Tennessee Studies in Literature, vol. 28. Knoxville, TN: University of Tennessee Press, pp. 131–147.

Buchan, David. (a) 1972. *The Ballad and the Folk*. London and Boston: Routledge and Regan Paul.

———. (b) 1978. "British Balladry: Medieval Chronology and Relations." In Otto Holzapfel, Julia McGraw and IØrn PiØ, eds., *The European Medieval Ballad: A Symposium*, Odense: Odense University Press, 1978, pp. 98–106.

Chambers, Edmund. 1945, 1964. *English Literature at the Close of the Middle Ages*. Oxford History of English Literature vol. 2, part 2. Oxford: Clarendon Press. 2nd edition 1964.

Child, Francis James, ed. 1883-98. *The English and Scottish Popular Ballads*, vols. I-V. Reissued 1962 by Cooper Square Publishers, New York, NY.

Cornelius, Roberta. 1931. "A New Text of an Old Ballad". *Publications of the Modern Language Association* 46: 1025–1033.

Deloney, Thomas. 1619. *The Pleasant Histoire of Iohn Winchcomb, in his Younger Years Called Iack of Newberie*. London: Humfrey Lowr es. Modern edition in F.O.Mann, ed., *The Works of Thomas Deloney*, Oxford: Clarendon Press, 1912.

Denholm-Young, N. 1969. *The Country Gentry in the Fourteenth Century*. Oxford: Clarendon Press.

Dobson, R.B. and J. Taylor. 1976. *Rymes of Robyn Hood: An Introduction to the English Outlaw*. London: Heinemann.

Dronke, Peter. 1968. *Die Lyrik des Mittelalters*. München: C.H.Beck.

Fowler, David C. 1968. *A Literary History of the Popular Ballad*. Durham, NC: Duke University Press.

Furnivall, Frederick J. 1890. *Captain Cox, His Ballads and Books; or, Robert Laneham's Letter*. Hertford: Stephen Austin and Sons, for the Ballad Society.

Garbaty, Thomas J. 1984. "Rhyme, Romance, Ballad, Burlesque, and the Confluence of Form". In Robert F. Yeager, ed., *Fifteenth-Century Studies*. Hamden, CT: Archon.

Greene, Richard Leighton, ed. 1935. *The Early English Carols*. Oxford: Clarendon Press. Reissued 1977.

Greimas, A.J. 1966. *Sémantique structurale*. Paris: Larousse.

Hales, John W. and Frederick J. Furnivall, eds. 1867–68. *Bishop Percy's Folio Manuscript: Ballads and Romances*. London: N. Trübner and Co.

Heffernan, Thomas J., ed. 1985. *The Popular Literature of Medieval England*. Tennessee Studies in Literature vol. 28. Knoxville, The University of Tennessee Press.

Hilton, R.H. 1958. "The Origins of Robin Hood". *Past and Present* 14: 30–44.

70

Hodgart, M.J.C. 1950, 1962. *The Ballads*. London: Hutchinson.

Holt, J.C. 1982. *Robin Hood*. London: Thames and Hudson.

Keen, Maurice. 1961. *The Outlaws of Medieval Legend*. London: Routledge and Kegan Paul.

A Lytell Geste of Robin Hode. Before 1519. London: Wynkin de Worde. Facsimile reprint by Theatrum Orbis Terrarum, Amsterdam, and Da Capo Press, New York, 1970.

Metzner, Ernst Erich. 1978. "Die mittelalterliche Volksballade im germanischen Raum unter besonderer Berücksichtigung des skandinavischen Nordens". In Willi Erzgräber, ed., *Europäische Spätmittelalter*. Neues Handbuch der Literaturwissenschaft vol. 8. Wiesbaden: Akademische Verlagsgesellschaft Athenaion, 331–354.

Morris, George 1948. "A Ryme of Robyn Hode". *Modern Language Review* 43: 507–508.

Müller, Wolfgand G. 1963. *Die englisch-schottische Volksballade*. Bern: F Rancke.

Murray, James A.H., ed. (a) 1872-73. *The Complaynte of Scotland*. Early English Text Society extra series 17 and 18. Reprinted 1973 by Kraus Reprints, Millwood, NY.

————, ed. (b) 1875. *The Romance and Prophecies of Thomas of Erceldoune*. Early English Text Society 61. London: N. Trübner.

Nixon, Ingeborg, ed. 1980. *Thomas of Erceldoune*. Publications of the Department of English, University of Copenhagen, vol. 9 part 1. Copenhagen: Akademisk Forlag.

Robertson, D.W. Jr. 1985. "Who Were 'The People'?" In Thomas J. Heffernan, ed., *The Popular Literature of Medieval England*. Tennessee Studies in Literature, vol. 28, Knoxville: The University of Tennessee Press, 3–29.

Rollins, Hyder E. 1919. "Concerning Bodelian Ms. Ashmole 48". *Modern Language Notes* 34: 340–351.

Stouck, Mary-Ann. 1981. "A Reading of the Middle English *Judas*". *Journal of English and Germanic Philology* 80: 188–198.

CHAPTER THREE

RECONSIDERING FOLK AND EPISODIC NARRATIVE

Mikle D. Ledgerwood

Let me begin by asking a question which quotes a critic of medieval literature and, I think, illustrates the need for a greater understanding of the import that structural, semiotic, and reader response criticism has for medieval narrative, especially epic and folk narratives.

Is it true that oral transmission "ineluctably le[a]ds to oversights and misunderstandings which contribute to the deterioration of the plot and the obfuscation of the original themes and structures" in medieval narratives and can these tales never "hope to attain the coherence and internal consistency of stories conceived and fashioned in one piece?" (Gantz: 13), or is this merely one way of looking at the differences between folk narrative and twentieth-century narrative, and not necessarily a helpful way of understanding folk narrative?

Such small items as the interchanging of minor characters' names and the accumulation of repetitive incidents can lead some modern critics to denigrate the structural unity that many folktales and other early medieval tales actually do possess. Some critics and especially Jeffrey Gantz, whom I am here quoting, believe that with folk narratives' overt emphasis on episodes, their refusal to adhere to a single central narrative line, their inclusion of many (perhaps unrelated) themes, and their lack of any clear macro-organizing principle hurt their sense of structural cohesiveness. (Gantz: 27)

This reading of medieval narrative structure is more than simply reading the past through present-colored glasses. It also expresses, through the mouths of critics who should know better, a misunderstanding of the purposes of folk narrative and a misapprehension of these "structural defects". As I have argued elsewhere, even these supposed defects can be eliminated by using structural and semiotic investigations into the role that character-function plays in joining the seams of episodic tales. I do not wish to restate again in a detailed fashion how this occurs, but I do wish to add how factors other than character-function seal seams in narratives and must be considered in terms of their anticipated reader response.

First and foremost, one must remember that oral narratives, just as any narrative, serve either to teach or to divert, and most often serve to do both. This is their purpose, not to uphold certain Victorian rules of structural integrity. Thus any inconsistency in details is irrelevant to their purpose, just as is the case in popular television today, where actors and characters' personalities change and where all parts of the world end up looking like Southern California. Secondly, as one would expect, medieval tales respond to their creators and their creators' societal needs and not to those of twentieth-century America (or nineteenth-century Europe). These told narratives were created to be appreciated by the listeners or (later) readers of their own epoch, and not by twentieth-century critics. Thus, it is to medieval society that we must look to understand more profoundly how these tales establish their own rules of structural cohesiveness and how through their intertextual nature they support a catholicity of communication between the texts' emitters and receivers.

One of the most important aspects of medieval European society, which is only now being duplicated in twentieth-century society, was its interrelationships which went far beyond national boundaries. With the Catholic Church being truly catholic and with Latin serving as an international form of communication, scholars could easily communicate by mail and in person, since all spoke the same language and shared some of the same cultural heritage. Many of the epistomological leaders of the church shared ideas as well, by traveling from one monastery or university to others, and especially to Rome. Thus, although we might know that St. Thomas Acquinas was English, that Richard of St. Victor was Scottish, that Pierre Abélard was French, and that Alfonso Sábio was Spanish, this knowledge is, for the most part, irrelevant. Medieval European thinkers were truly pan-European, or at least pan-Christian in their writing and thought.

Many medieval writers and performers of narratives shared this disinterest in royal or noble political boundaries. Although their works were most often performed in the Vulgar tongues of Europe rather than the high language of Latin, they were still part of the open, Catholic, Europe. It is well-known that many troubadours, trouvères, and Minnesänger traveled to courts in various parts of Europe. These performers would often sing poems and songs in languages or dialects foreign to their audiences, much in the way that opera is performed in the United States today. Some of these same performers and others were masters of several foreign languages and dialects. They were able to translate narratives into the language of their audience with, one would imagine, varying amounts of success.

By this time it should be clear that Medieval European society was very closely interrelated in political, social, and most importantly, cultural and religious terms. It is only natural, then, that all written texts from the medieval period should share in this interrelation, that they should reflect the similarity of circumstances and thought of their creators, or that they should show a very important part of their nature to be intertextual. Now only were they influenced by other works from their period and earlier centuries, they also often wrote part of those other works into their own structure, with this interrelatedness being most evident in scholarly works that did include parts of other writers' works. Plagiarism, as C.S. Lewis has pointed out was not viewed as the same moral wrong that it is today.

In the same way as plagiarism of semantic content, story-tellers of the medieval period did not consider plagiarism of similar structures to be an issue to be considered at all. In non-scholarly works that were written to tell a story for didactic purposes (or essentially all medieval narratives) similarities are obvious, whether the narratives were lives of the saints, tales of chivalric heroes or tales of larger-than-life mythic heroes. These texts arising out of the oral tradition then should be considered as complex signs that are intertextual in nature. All literary scholars now recognize that to say that literature is intertextual is tautologous. Yet in medieval oral-inspired narratives, intertextuality has a specific role to play. In a larger sense, one could say that many medieval fictive works are essentially composed of interrelated constructs that accomplish differing didactic goals through the same narrative means instead of saying that they are essentially culture-connected constructs accomplishing their didactic goals through inadequate structural methods. However, let us prove this contention by examining some narratives to see whether they are composed of interrelated constructs. They we can decide to what purpose this intertextuality occurred and what it says about narrative in general, at least in a medieval sense.

Let us take a number of early medieval texts, all of which are probably rather well-known, including *La Chanson de Roland*, the Saints' lives of St. Alexis and Ste. Marguerite, and certain Welsh tales from the *Mabinogion*. Other tales such as any of the *romans courtois* or the *Lais* of Marie de France or Germanic folk narratives could have been used. However the range included in these texts should be sufficient to analyze the type of reader-text interaction that takes place and show how this interaction is fundamentally similar even in purportedly dissimilar texts.

To give a brief summary of each group is probably necessary here. Let us give outlines of each text and show their didactic purpose to their medieval readers or listeners. *La Chanson de Roland* is primarily a text outlining the code of chivalric honor. The protagonist, Roland, represents the flower of medieval knighthood. He is immensely strong and skilled at combat. Yet the poet has the last word when Roland's overweening pride and his lack of wisdom leads to his own death and the death of thousands of his men. In fact, it is only through the encouragement of his friend, Olivier, that Roland brings Charlemagne and ensures (ultimately) the avenging of his death. The principal lesson taught here is that no matter how admirable or debonnaire Roland may be, his time on Earth has brought about ruin through his lack of humility, an important Christian virtue. It is only in his humbling of himself to blow his horn that any kind of non-tragic end can occur in the narrative. For a society that valued force-at-arms so highly, this lesson must indeed be deemed an important and necessary one.

In its structure, the tale moves linearly forward to the ultimate drawing and quartering of the traitor, Ganelon. It does include, however, some simultaneous action which is described sequentially, with the device of furthering the anticipation of the semantic *Stoff* to follow. Along with some description of emotions and occurrences, however briefly presented, that stop the plot from continuing along its merry syntagmatic way.

The Saints' lives of St. Alexis and Ste. Marguerite are narratives that emphasize the importance of total faith and submission to God. Both protagonists must overcome their own initial reluctance to believe in the God speaking to them; they must also overcome the desires of their own flesh and family, and of course the physical pain and the death which defines their martyrdom. This type of tale is especially important for the Church, which often needed more than just the ancient examples to convince and convert. The saints are people from more recent eras. They were often aristocrats whose families resembled aristocratic families of the early medieval period. Thus their lives were *exempla* that hit much harder and much closer to home than the *exempla* of the church fathers, most of whom came from poorer families and almost all of whom were Jewish. These newer saints were non-Semitic characters with whom the medieval aristocrat could more easily identify. As converts preaching Christian virtues from aristocratic Roman (or European) families these saints would provide an effective role-model for the aristocracy concerning the importance of humility and of helping the church.

The structure of these tales is more sophisticated, as it shows circularity by beginning with a physical birth and ending with a moral rebirth through the characters' death. Yet essentially, the stories include an introduction to the problems of martyrdom, an exposition or development of the character and situation, the death of the character, and finally the miracles and the ascension to sainthood. Just as with the *Chanson de Roland* an episodic nature predominates. The unity of the story, based on a rigid formula, is quite strong, yet the episodes vary greatly in their length and details.

The last group of Welsh legends and adventures include groups of narratives which can be associated with either the *Chanson de Roland* or the saints' lives in terms of their moral and didactic purposes. A thirteenth century version of Welsh folktales and legends, called the *Mabinogion* for short, comprises a great variety of stories, some of which involve the supernatural and the færie world, some of which do not. Yet if we were to characterize this loosely connected series of tales, most of them have a moral or didactic purpose.

Many of the collections' stories such as those of Mallolwch, Gwydion, and Maxen tell of the problems that greed and duplicity will eventually bring to wrong-doers. Others (and many of the same ones) speak of the chivalric code of honor and the importance of moral force as an adjunct to physical force. Another group, including the story of Rhiannon, tell of the eventual righting of wrong and the importance of not following blindly superstitious feelings. In fact, the punishment of foolishness, reckless pride, and avarice are all central points of the stories of Pryderi, Manawydan, and Pwyll whereas in the stories of Owein and Gereint (see also the stories of Yvain and Guerin in the tales of Chrétien de Troyes) the central focus revolves around the struggle between the duties of marriage and the duties of a career (here that of a knight errant). In fact in almost all of the stories called together the *Mabinogion*, the central focus is the didactic teaching of goodness and virtue as more important than simple physical strength and force-at-arms.

It is these stories, however, that Gantz was discussing as possessing structural inadequacies. Here, it is often the force of character-function which is the only seam that runs through some of the stories. Nevertheless, setting and recurrent didactic themes, as we will see, also unify these stories in the same way as the earlier two groups.

After considering a summary of these three groups of texts, it appears that they represent most of the genres of early medieval fictive writing in languages other than Latin, yet they are involved in the same semiotic communication and much more similar, structurally and semantically, than a first reading might indicate. Although considered to be fiction by twentieth-century readers, each author of each of these works believed that his main purpose was to present his own account of events that he felt had occurred, or a basically historical account. The study of history has always served didactic purposes, and these accounts prove to be no different, with their underlying intent being to instruct the religiously-supported aristocracy previously defined. Yet these texts are not crudely didactic in the sense of a catechism or a list of commandments. They are literary texts and thus involve the notion of literary truth as well as moral and historical truth. In the case of these texts, the moral and historical truths are arrived at from a literary path. These texts are structured so the reader (and penultimately the hearer) can perceive these truths only by completing the journey that perusing the text requires.

As non-semiotic literary critics often forget, the path followed to reach the end of a text or the means of textual communication is often as important as the message communicated in a literary work. In fact it is only by investigating the procedure of how the message is communicated that the message's interpretants can be understood. Thus the way that a particular truth or goal is reached is an essential part of that goal and perhaps explains part of the repetitiveness and similarity in the episodes of these texts by giving to the author(s) a desire to render the path more familiar to his or her readers/listeners. This, of course, would ensure that the receiver would be more able to follow the text due to its familiarity. This type of method employing familiar repeated episodes and linear structures is still used successfully by authors of romance and gothic novels.

For some works of literature, especially popular works, their didactic goal and their sociological function may not be automatically evident, just as a walk along the beach often has no directly obvious goal except the enjoyment of the scenery one passes. These works may have no intended function except the enjoyment of the text as one peruses it. Nevertheless, we would agree, I propose, that greater literary works of art also promote new understandings of important social, moral, ethical, or existential questions—that they make us see the world that we live in in a new light through their created worlds of the text.

This is what these medieval works are doing for readers both modern and contemporary. They are taking us beyond the level of the popular story and subtly encouraging more involved readings aiming at a more prolonged consideration of the interpretants aimed at their receivers. All three macrotexts here presented take their users into their own world. For medieval readers or listeners this was a world familiar to them—one in which Christian morals and ethics were the normal background of their lives, but also one in which the older pagan beliefs still played a part. It was a world full of violence and war, of jealousy and fear, yet one in which a code of honor and action had to be followed if one wished to avoid disasterous consequences. Only through the understanding of this world, as aided through the creation of texts, could one hope to understand one's real mission in this cosmos. Thus the texts of this cosmos had to be both æsthetically interesting and familiar enough to encourage their followers to use them. They also had to be endowed with enough truth and teaching to encourage the path's caretakers, the storytellers, to keep it open and unobstructed.

The rules of the path-game and essentially the search for the end-game are quite clear. First, in terms of the tales' characters, there is a central character whose actions must be followed through a story. In the case of a long tale, such as the *Chanson de Roland* or the *Vie de St. Alexis*, the spoor of the central hero continues long beyond his death as other characters take up his trace and act according to the requirements that his actions have already established. Secondly, there are a host of secondary characters that act either as evil characters in opposition to the good deeds of the central hero, as good characters in opposition to the egotistical acts of the central hero, or in concert with the good acts of the central hero.

Thirdly, the tales' plots all involve a series of situations in which the characters find themselves, the situations being linked by the use of the same characters or perhaps by a central quest or motivating force. The episodes that spring from the plot then all return to the motivating character and his need for experience and instruction. Even the episodes that seem extraneous or irrelevant have the purpose of building up the larger-than-life aspects of the central character, both his good points to be emulated and his flaws to be studied and avoided. They are, as a result, adventures that exist to reinforce the receiver's impression of the dominant central character.

In addition, this reinforcement by the piling up of episodes is a very important part of making sure that the message is not lost. As social psychologists, communications scientists and semioticians have discovered, the possibility of receiving an inaccurate message is much greater in the oral transmission of a text. Without being able to reread a text, the oral listener needs additional and repetitive information to be sure that the entropy level inherent in oral transmission is low. Therefore, in the original, oral, transmission of these tales, episodes and attributes had to be repeated so that the central characteristics of the tale were intensified and clarified.

An additional aid to the listener's reception of a message is that often a tale's general outline would be familiar to him or her before it was told in this particular incarnation. When this is true, the rules of characters and episodes are pre-determined before the game begins. The individual tale differs in its detailing, in its names and locations, and in the æsthetic skill of its teller, yet the message produced becomes on the one hand a familiar didactic one in which the listener is placed into his/her societal and cosmological context and is encouraged to accept the nature of his society's basis; whereas on the other hand, this familiarity also entices the receiver into paying more attention to the particular telling of a tale, to see how its unique performance can æsthetically underline certain attributes and understandings by the variations in the texts.

Thus medieval texts go beyond the extended metaphor of a path to be followed docilely and single-mindedly by its users. Since the destination of the path is *often* familiar before the journey is begun, since the underlying intertextual rules are definitely familiar to all parts of the audience, and since the interrelatedness of the society and culture as a whole unites the audience, the texts encourage their users, both emitters and receivers, to help create new forks of the path and *perhaps* even new destinations. They establish in an open-ended fashion a dialogue in which anticipated reader-reaction plays an important part in the text's transfer of knowledge and understanding. The reader, while enjoying the process of information dissemination and obtaining a feeling of accomplishment at the end of the literary peregrination, can obtain this enjoyment only through an understanding of the rules of the journey and the communicatory dialogue. He/She must be aware of his/her role as interpreters of the text, and especially the affective role of the audience on the text. It is well-known that audiences do not choose to sit still through a badly-told or boring story. Abuse of many kinds would accompany a bad performance. Thus stories would be adapted to avoid this type of reaction. Didactic purposes would be made more acceptable, æsthetic norms would not be allowed to be violated, and more verisimilitude in the sense of concrete details would be added to help draw listeners further into this world.

Yet it must not be thought that these tales were created out of total chaos in anarchy, or even worse, in committee. Each time a tale was told in an oral manner, it was created anew; but it was always created by a single teller, even if the teller were influenced by his/her receivers. The creator of the tales is still the creator. He or She would respond to all types of stimuli and influence but would respond through his/her own understanding, intent, and gifts. In the case of tales told so often that we know that a series of authors and audiences must have created them, the version that is recorded in a written fashion is simply one creation of a series of creations, perhaps better or perhaps worse told in this incarnation. We also know certainly that the tales are less vividly told without the complex vocal and kinesic signs that an oral taleteller has at his/her command.

Thus in this sense, these oral tales are open-ended. Nevertheless, this open-endedness does not degenerate into confusion or Babel (babble). The tales follow the rules of the game. The narratives do end. They do, for the most part, have a linear structure whose syntagmatic nature is not in question although they can be multifaceted with the myriad forks and occasional backtracking that their structure presents. What they also do, however, is present their audience with test cases of Christian/Chivalric behaviour. Each episode or anecdote serves a didactic purpose, even if a limited one; and each repeated episode with little variation of theme or semantic content obviously reinforces these lessons. Those protagonists who succeed according to the rules of the moral and æsthetic episodes of the poet will be the characters who must be emulated. Even when the protagonist and many other characters are dead by the end of the work, the morally successful character is vindicated through his after-life or by being avenged by a character helped by God.

The death of the hero has been, again, often discussed and treated by critics. Yet for us here this end emphasizes the open ending of most of these tales, whose heroes end in heaven or Avalon. Once again, these serve to remind us that in medieval society it was obvious to everyone that human existence was merely transitory. Heaven, Hell, or Purgatory was the next step in existence and even Purgatory is merely a step towards redemption or rejection. Thus medieval terrestrial life by this single fact shows its open-endedness in its very essence, as these tales reflect.

Therefore, the importance of characters, episodes, and their constant revision and renewal reveals to us a society whose end was well-known, yet whose path and means to get there was constantly being reviewed in an open-ended yet carefully coded manner to explain the journey in its most rewarding æsthetic possibility. It also reveals to us a society whose understanding of the intertextual or pantextual rules of didactic narrative shows clearly how the game was to be played justly and fairly by the tales' emitters or receivers, as any of the text's heroes themselves certainly would know how to do.

REFERENCES

Gantz, Jeffrey, ed. 1975. *The Mabinogion.* Yale University Press.

Ledgerwood, Mikle D. (a) 1982. "Character-Function in Romanian Folk Ballads." *Romance Notes*: 52-57.

————. (b) 1987. "A Comparison of the Use of Narrative Character-Function in Romanian Folk Ballads and the *Lais* of Marie de France." *Semiotica* 63-1/2: 163-169.

Lewis, C.S. 1964. *The Discarded Image, An Introduction to Medieval and Renaissance Literature.* Cambridge: Cambridge University Press.

CHAPTER FOUR

THE DRAMA OF THE SIGN: THE SIGNS OF THE DRAMA

SunHee Kim Gertz

One of the more fruitful areas for semiotic investigation is drama, as seems particularly apparent in medieval drama. Besides the broader literary theoretical questions posed by any playscript, such as "what is the text?" and "who are its 'readers'?," drama elicits specifically semiotic questions. In order to analyze drama, for example, it is necessary to consider how performance creates meaning. Through the investigation of this and other problems, our understanding of relationships among meaning, language, and visible signs can deepen. The semiotic problem I will be addressing here is how language and staging can extend a play's meaning, as seen in the theatrical modification of conventional signs.

It may seem unneccessarily problematic to make theatrical elements central, while concomitantly limiting my inquiry to an instance of medieval drama. Our knowledge of acting troupes, performances, and staging areas during the period is, at best, sketchy, (Ogden: 63-66).[1] Medievalists, however, often make a virtue of necessity. Thus, rather than exploring the vast scope mapped out by Keir Elam in *The Semiotics of Theatre and Drama*, scholars of medieval drama must rely largely on textual evidence. This particular limit does serve as a virtue, though, since it in effect eliminates some major theoretical difficulties. For example, in his study, Elam distinguishes the performance text—that which occurs in the theater—from the dramatic text—essentially, the playscript—providing, of course, for overlaps between the two categories. He thereby articulates a highly useful distinction, but goes on to argue that the performance text should take into account different productions as well as variables such as stages, actors, costuming, and performances. This seems a task more useful, however, to a director deliberating on the staging of an individual play rather than to a theorist trying to come to terms with how drama generates meaning. In any theoretical consideration, a streamlining or generalizing process must occur; accidents such as different theatrical spaces or a single actor's various performances can be effectively ignored for critical theatrical elements. In any case, more important for semiotic analysis here is the fact that medieval religious drama is quintessentially textual: it stages biblical narratives, thereby three-dimensionalizing literary texts that themselves are understood to signify another text, God's creation and its message of salvation (see Gellrich).

The distinct logocentricism of texts surviving from the middle ages makes language theory an important and ubiquitous cultural strand. Semiotic investigation is particularly useful under these conditions, since the period's major philosophical texts along with their application in less complex vehicles, like sermons or stained glass windows, themselves rely on sign theory. In addition to highlighting signs and their meanings, medieval drama plays upon a relatively uniform set of conventions. For this study, the value of these conventions resides not so much in their signification, which scholars have amply written upon, but in *how* drama relies upon them to generate meaning. In addition, the particular play used here to explore these dynamics, the Digby *Mary Magdalene*, not only modifies conventions to generate meaning, it also crystallizes how readers (or viewers) in this literary system may interpret signs.[2]

The Digby *Mary Magdalene*, probably written in late fifteenth century East Anglia, survives in only one manuscript, the MS Digby 133, but it is also one of the extant medieval playscripts that contains numerous stage directions (see Baker for edition used). Fortunately, these directions along with what we know of medieval drama provide enough material to delve into the probable impact of performances on its audiences, which include various levels of a village or town's population (see Coldewey and Kindermann). With no fixed theater, audiences are likely to have viewed the play as set up on the village green or town square, its make-shift stages thus forming unstable frameworks, since the playing spaces would be constructed only to be "de-constructed" later. In the Digby play, the playing space includes platforms (of an uncertain number) and areas between them that altogether represent the forces of Hell, the World, and Heaven.[3] Despite the lack of a fixed theater, then, the playing space itself has fixed meaning, a fundamental condition allowing semiotic inquiry.

The theatrical transformation of common village or town spaces into a stage representing the universe is underscored by the material of the play.[4] Magdalene, a daughter of the ruler Cyrus, journeys from birth in sin to maidenly decorum only to fall into sin, a fall that is followed by her redemption and final embracing of Christ. Thus, she moves from profane to sacred, uniting in her person the profane and sacred uses of the playing space. Moreover, her life is presented as the journey of Everyperson, as inferred, for example, by the fact that all, even Christ, are dramatically subordinate to her (Bennett: 7). At the same time, her life is depicted as dependent upon and interwoven with Christ's, in effect, viewing the resurrection play (which ordinarily focuses on Christ)[5] from the margins, not unlike the perspective impelling *Rosencrantz and Guildenstern Are Dead*.[6] Further unifying the play while implying her importance, the Digby play apocryphally conflates biblical narratives in the single person of Magdalene: she becomes the favored one of Christ who anoints his feet, the one from whom Christ expelled seven devils, as well as the one to whom Christ first appeared upon his resurrection [see Baker: xl, and Grantly (c)].

Magdalene *is* Everyperson, not only in her redemption, emblematic relation to Christ, and dramatic and unifying centrality, but also in her being caught between profane and sacred powers, whose differences are made apparent in their language (Baker: xxxv, xlvii.). Thus, the beginning of the play is firmly fixed in the world, as Tiberius, Pilate, and Herod vaunt their power with alliterative bombast. Upon her redemption and turning to Christ's kingdom, however, light-filled references and symbols punctuate the play (in language and on stage, as directions indicate). This linguistically anchored contrast is further nuanced by how the playing space is used, as can be seen in Magdalene's movements.[7] Before her fall, for example, she is characterized somewhat statically as a maiden of the romance genre, "ful fayur and ful of femynyte" (71). When her father Cyrus dies, however, Magdalene immerses herself in the pleasures of the world, a fall associated with lack of forward movement: after her stay in a tavern, she falls asleep in an arbor. Finally, in the latter part of the play, her redeemed state is conveyed through apostolically impelled action: a journey by ship, a contest with pagans, a procession in light, travels with the Queen of Marseilles, and ascension into heaven after thirty years in the wilderness.

Similarly enhancing the redemption narrative are the play's typological references, references also common in hagiography. The fallen part of a saint's life, for example, may be made to relate to the antetype of Eve or Adam, while the redeemed part of a saint's life may be made to relate to the type of the Virgin Mary or Christ (see Charity). In a sense, typology conflates figurative language (such as the rulers' bombastic commands and the references to light) with staged action or movement, since it assigns *narrative* value (a chain of events, action) to images (figured vehicles). As such, this signing system is indeed present in the Digby play, inferring the entire salvation story not only by Magdalene's postlapsarian lethargy in the arbor, but also, notably, in references that link her with the Virgin. Thus, when the King and Queen of Marseilles thank Magdalene for her help, they call upon her maiden purity with phrases associated with the Virgin:

> [Queen]: *O virgo salutata*, for ower savacyon!
> *O pulcra et casta*, cum of nobyll alyavns!
> O almyty Maydyn, ower sowlys confortacyon! [...]
> Heyll, þou chosyn and chast of wommen alon!
> (1899–1943)

Considering Magdalene's life, such salutations must be taken figuratively, and thus in addition to signifying the salvation story, these lines signal the contrast between her worldly and spiritual lives. In doing so, they also suggest a life or narrative valued more for its action than for its language (ultimately, a metadramatic message, as discussed in more detail below).

Thus, the story of redemption—underscored by the play's figurative language, movement, and typological references—transforms the playing area framing Magdalene's life into a figuratively dense space. Indeed, the playing space conveys the entire scope of history as experienced by *humankind* from a perspective that is understood to be *divine*. Expressed another way, by juxtaposing scenes from various parts of the universe and by using figural conventions such as the Eve-Mary types, vast expanses of space and time are traversed, enabling the playing space to signify a mortal rendition of the timelessness experienced by God alone.[8] For, as Boethius writes in his *Consolatio Philosophiae*, the entire stretch of human history from God's perspective is located in the eternal present. Chaucer renders one of Philosophia's passages in this manner:

> Semblable thing is it, that the resoun of mankynde ne weneth nat
> that the devyne intelligence byholdeth or knoweth thingis to
> comen, but ryght as the resoun of mankynde knoweth hem [...] the
> prescience of God seeth alle thinges certeins and diffinyssched,
> althoughe thei ne han no certein issues or by tydyngis..."
> (V. Prosa 5 76-104, see Benson for edition used)

Semiotic density, then, informs the basic framework of the play. Since it is also steeped in widely known conventions, the Digby playwright can count on knowledge that will enable him or her to explore God's text more deeply and to generate new meanings. More specifically, since the play communicates in a literary system that recognizes the signing power of language not only as the basis of communication but also as a portal to salvation, the Digby playwright can and, I contend, does take semiotic inquiry further than simple recognition of the world as an instance of God's language.

To begin with, in representing Everyperson, Magdalene functions as a sign, an instance of a greater pattern.[9] To view Magdalene in this way, however, the audience must respond to the play in loosely Augustinian terms. Thus, as articulated in *De Doctrina Christiana*,[10] the world is God the Author's text, and every aspect of this richly diverse text is an instance of his language, complete with semiotic impact.[11] But when the culmination of God's creation, humankind, fell through the disobedience of the first couple, humans (instances of God's words), as well as human language, acquired multiple levels of meaning, variance, and lost their primordial univocal meanings (as conveyed in the antetype of Babel). God's creatures as well as their words can, however, redeem that mutable state of their lives and language through redirecting their lives to God (as conveyed in the type of the Pentecost).[12]

Magdalene suggests loosely Augustinian thought when telling her siblings of her conversion, doing so linguistically, but in spatial terms, "Grace to me he wold nevyr denye;/ Thowe I were nevyr so synful, he seyd, 'Revertere'!" (756–757). Thus, the Augustinian admonition to return to the original relationship between God and humankind becomes a gestural, physical movement that, in effect, creates a spatial metaphor—through words—inferring the moral realignment necessary to achieve spiritual cleansing. Of course, this spatial metaphor could be emphasized on stage by physical movement. More importantly, it is linked to the common metaphor of life as a pilgrimage, an extension of meaning not difficult for an audience familiar with pilgrimages as well as with the stations of the cross to make. Indeed, the Digby playwright dramatizes this particular link as well. As indicated earlier, prior to her decision to turn to Christ, Magdalene did not move much, thereby echoing the rulers of the world, like the King of Marseilles, who are viewed as securely ensconced on their platforms. However, like Magdalene, the King of Marseilles does experience conversion, upon which, he begins to echo Christ, the true ruler, who moves throughout the play; that is, the King makes an "actual" pilgrimage with Peter through the stations of the cross (1847–1850), a journey emphasized by the parallel pilgrimage taken by his supposedly dead wife, who is accompanied by Magdalene (1903–1910).[13]

In this manner, the Digby playwright attaches physical and narrative movement to the metaphor of turning to the good and suggests that life in Christ means development, while life in the world means stasis and stagnation. Moreover, alerted to the idea of redemption by the term *revertere* and to the pilgrimage by the staged journeys of the Rulers of Marseilles, viewers may be further led to delve more deeply into the relations between mortals and language. That is, the staging of the active Christian life as a pilgrimage when viewed through the perspective of Augustinian semiotics suggests that such a pilgrimage is actually *not* figurative; it is literal, since mortals *are* instances of God's words. What is figurative to mortals is literal to God.

In semiotic terms, staging generates a figurative depiction, a synecdoche of the world. In the Digby play, moreover, the synecdochal depiction of Magdalene's life is further underscored as the play translates linguistic figures of speech—the pilgrimage, for example—into action. When viewed through a theological lens, the act of presenting a figure of speech as a concrete reality mirrors God's creation, which also translated his words into the world. The deeper significance of *divine* language, then, can become evident through working out *mortal* language's various levels in time and space, thereby suggesting that drama can be an ideal vehicle for this message. Thus, the Digby playwright suggests the value of mortal language in the actions it accomplishes—the blustery commands of the rulers "go" nowhere, whereas Christ's single *"Revertere"* unleashes a chain of events that keeps Magdalene in motion.

The Digby playwright further suggests drama as an ideal vehicle for conveying this message by associating language with the ability to confuse, thereby necessitating that language be evaluated, or interpreted, in terms of action. Thus, the play first refers to *variance* in the initial scene, where the word is used to mean "discrepancy." The emperor Tiberius will not condone any who are at "weryouns" with him; rather, he will condemn them to "mordor and myschanse!" (36–39). The next reference to *variance* means "a condition contrary to stability" or "mutability." Magdalene's brother, Lazarus, thanks their father Cyrus for the inheritance he bestows upon them and their sister Martha, and hopes that the three children may so live as to "...haue joye wythowtyn weryauns" (92). Later on, the Queen of Marseilles uses "dyversyte" in the same way to praise her husband, who keeps her from the diversity of sorrow; that is, he creates a constant environment of joy for her (955).

Notably, these three examples connote a negative attitude to change or multiplicity, yet each of them recognizes its negative impact only within the worldly rather than within the spiritual framework. Although the words *variance* and *diversity* indicate something negative, language is not perfect enough to pinpoint the actual problem.[14] Magdalene becomes aware of this confusion when the Good Angel reprimands her as follows:

> Woman, woman, why art *p*ou so onstabyll?
> Ful bytterly thys blysse it wol be bowth!
> Why art *p*ou a3ens God *so veryabyll*? [...]
> Salue for *p*i sowle must be sowth,
> And leve *p*i werkys wayn and *veriabyll*! [...]
> Remembyr *p*e on mercy, *make pi sowle clyre*!
> (588–600, my italics)

Having succumbed to the *blysse*-ful language of Curiosity and Lechery, Magdalene finally learns they use the ambiguity of language to mask that her actions proclaim her as allied to the world, while the Good Angel uses ambiguous words (as in *blysse*) to direct her clearly and without ambiguity to God. Forsaking the mutability of the world, her turning, *revertere*, is coupled with this recognition and signals a shift to a different set of images. Magdalene understands now that variance is darkness, and true stability is signified through the clarity, the light offered by God's perfect word, Christ.[15]

The Digby playwright thus weaves conventional material associated with Christian commonplaces to deepen the figurative dimension of the play—variance and darkness are coupled in contrast to stability and light, and all resonates with conventional Christian associations. Moreover, these contrasts highlight the creative use of the redemption story dominating the play. Macroscopically, the play moves from the forces of the world to the force of Christ, from the multiple rulers to the single ruler. But, in addition, the redemption story is repeated microscopically throughout the play: Magdalene's fall is redeemed by her turning to Christ, Cyrus's death in the world is contrasted with Lazarus's death and subsequent rescue by Christ's calling him forth from the darkness of the tomb into the light of day, and the King and Queen of Marseilles begin in the world only to be redeemed through Magdalene, who appears to them in a passage brimming with light imagery. In other words, redemption not only informs the overall linear structure of the play, as emphasized by its variance-light imagery, its dynamics are reiterated, linearly and non-linearly, throughout the play.[16]

These dynamics not only deepen the play's figurative and structural meaning. In addition, they allow images to play against one another, thereby further complicating the play's semiotic texture and creating metadramatic levels in the process. Upon first viewing, the way the metadramatic works in the Digby play is, perhaps, not evident, since it is closer to the type of meta*literary* dynamics that pervade Homer's *Odyssey*, as exemplified through Athena's patronage of Odysseus, than to more traditionally understood metadramatic conventions, such as those in Shakespeare's plays within plays. When we learn, for example, that as part of her overall plan, Athena wishes to make her hero particularly attractive so he might win over Nausicaa, daughter of the King of the Phaeacians, Homer depicts Athena as making her hero taller and stronger, while making his locks curl like the hyacinth, and then compares her work to that of an artisan trained by herself and Hephaestus (see Murray for edition used). A simple interpretation of this passage implies that wisdom becomes Odysseus. On the metaliterary level, however, the scene documents reflections on artistry, as signalled by the reference to Hephaestus. Thus, one such metaliterary reflection might conclude that wisdom and artistry must coalesce to have the desired effect on audiences, as inferred by Homer's associating

Hephaestus' pleasing artifacts with Odysseus' highly crafted linguistic artifacts. In other words, the passage extends the narrative by creating a subtle metaliterary level, the exploration of which is sparked by the quasi-allegorical nature of Athena's presence.

The way the metaliterary works in the Homeric scene may be used to comment on how the metadramatic works in the Digby play. To begin with, the play makes its language reflect its action, as exemplified by the use of the language of variance and light in conjunction with the movement from sin to redemption. The echoing of language and action, furthermore, is repeated time and again, suggesting, among other things, its importance to the playwright. These conditions allow the metadramatic to be generated, as can be explored by looking at the play's Edenic allusions.

When Curiosity or Pride besieges Magdalene with sweet words, allegorical readings are encouraged just as they are when Athena anoints her hero. Watching Magdalene move to the arbor from her castle further suggests the initial temptation and the loss of Eden, which then also typologically foreshadows the paradise promised by God. The conflation of Eden and its eschatalogical associations with Magdalene's worldly arbor moreover recalls the timelessness that characterizes God's language. This dense use of the arbor becomes metadramatic when attention is turned to how the play's language mirrors its actions. When Magdalene falls, for example, her language becomes sensuous.[17] Later, when turned to the proper "grom of blysse" (489)—not the taverner she addresses here—her sensual love is transformed into spiritual love; she learns to read God's text properly. Indeed, Christ teaches her how to read God's transformed language by picking up on the Edenic allusions. Thus, in the *Hortulanus* scene, upon Magdalene's surprise for having mistaken her Lord for the gardener, Christ answers:

> So I am, forsothe, Mary!
> Mannys hartt is my gardyn here.
> Perin I sow sedys of vertu all þe 3ere.
> Þe fowle wedys and wycys I reynd vp be þe rote!
> Whan þat gardyn is watteryd wyth terys clere,
> Than spryng vertuus, and smelle full sote.
> (1080-1085)

The lesson here, that Christ redeems Eden, builds upon the typological dynamics that link Eden and paradise by taking the common vehicle—the garden—and literalizing it into *portrayed* action (sowing, weeding, watering), as will be achieved later, three-dimensionally, with the pilgrimages (described above).   In addition, Christ teaches Magdalene how to read in a manner that reflects his pedagogical method in the Scriptures, where he uses parables, that also figuratively equate a short narrative with an underlying message.   By making action the determining signifier, the Digby playwright also makes clear that complex lessons require *experienced* readers.   Indeed, earlier, Christ attempted to teach the disciples to read through his resurrection of Lazarus: "of my deth shew yow I wyll" (856).   But the lesson remained an enigma to them, a foreshadowing in God's text of later events, which can only be understood in its full significance after having *experienced* the interpretive key.

Importantly, the deepening of Magdalene's understanding by her experience and Christ's use of figuratively portrayed action comments upon how a play works, as is underscored by her reference to the Pentecost shortly before she is to board ship for Marseilles, "Of alle maner tonggys he 3af vs knowyng,/ For to vndyrstond every langwage" (1343–1344).   As inferred by the juxtaposition of the reference to her journey, the Pentecost suggests that language can redeem through, paradoxically, the negation of its surface level—the part of language that causes confusion—and the refusal to dwell in any one space.   Magdalene was ravished by Curiosity and Pride's sensual language which generated her own confused language and deadly sleep, and she was awakened by Christ's dramatizing of God's message in language.

In this sense, human linguistic creativity is aligned metadramatically with action.   The playwright further explores this idea creatively by means of a well-known Christian convention, the wine and bread which in the New Testament, Christ transforms into a metaphor for his blood and body at the last supper.   Through modifying this commonplace, the playwright establishes a metadramatic *leitmotif*.[18]

Wine is used repeatedly in the play in combination with spices at banquet scenes to connote conviviality.[19]   These references demonstrate the abuse of God's formerly univalent signs by translating their purposes into mutable worldly activities.

Tiberius, Cyrus, and the unredeemed King of Marseilles, for example, call for wine and spices before sitting down to banquets. That seems harmless enough, but after Cyrus's death, an important gloss on the play's use of wine occurs. Magdalene accepts Lechery as her "hartys leche" (461) and enters a tavern, another setting for conviviality. The taverner advertises his great variety of wines and then addresses Magdalene:

> Here, lady, is wyn, a repast,
> To man and woman a good restoratyff.
> 3e xall nat thynk your mony spent in wast—
> From stodyys and hevynes it woll yow relyff!
> (485–488)

Through their wording, these lines deliberately suggest a profane contrast to the wine of the eucharist. Significantly, the next scene also portrays a banquet, Simon's banquet for Christ and his followers, the banquet where Magdalene is redeemed and where wine very easily could have been used. Wine, however, is not mentioned during the entire scene. Instead, we are confronted with words dealing with consolation, substance, food, and restoratives. In other words, this scene focuses on the bread that is the body of Christ, and forms a contrast to the other, worldly, banquet scenes.

The profane banquet emphasizes wine, while the sacred banquet emphasizes sustenance and food. Keeping with these contrasts, the playwright makes bread emphasize spiritual sustenance throughout the play. The Good Angel, for example, prays to Christ in gratitude for Magdalene's salvation, "And wyth your gostely bred to fede vs, we desyern" (721). The King of Marseilles laments that his child will die "...for defawth of sustynons" (1769). But, as later narrated by the Queen, Magdalene saved the Queen and the child as she cared for their sustenance (1902–1905), and the King praises the Lord as "[t]he helth of ower sowllys, and repast contemplatyff!" (1940). Finally, in the last scene set in the wilderness, this bread "literally" becomes Magdalene's bread of life, which Christ has sent her through his angels.[20]

This creation of new stage symbolism through modifying Christian commonplaces is achieved by the narrative playing out of the action in drama, not unlike how Christ literalizes the garden topos linguistically.[21] In time, the audience can conflate the two parts of this commonplace, not unlike how, in time, the disciples will understand that Lazarus was intended as a foreshadowing of Christ's own resurrection. Drama, in other words, clarifies mysteries. More importantly, however, drama can renew the sense of wonder sometimes lost when a convention is too well known. Thus, having established this modifying and theatrical set of signs, the Digby playwright intensifies and revives their visible aspect as signs. In the conversion of the King and Queen of Marseilles, for example, food and sustenance imagery is combined with light imagery to affirm the truth of God's message. In particular, after the pagan temple is destroyed by fire through Magdalene's prayer, the King requests that the royal couple might conceive a child through God's grace in exchange for their conversion to Christianity (1571-1574). Magdalene agrees, but what she prays for, at least on the literal level, varies with her intention:

> Now, Cryst, my creatur, me conserve and kepe,
> Þat I be natt confunddyd with þis reddure!
> For hungore and thurst to þe I wepe! [...]
> Good Lord, so hellpe me and sokore,
> Lord, as itt is þi hye pleseawns!
> (1578–1585)

Christ acts, saying that he will supply her "...wyth sustinons corporall" (1589). Then, however, Magdalene is instructed to put on white clothing and appear to the King with two angels and candles (a metadramatic instance in the Shakespearean sense), with Christ acting as stage manager to the action that follows. She does so, but tells the King that she has "...hongor, threst, and chelle" (1613). The day dawns, and the King and Queen relate their visions to one another, resulting in the King's summons of Magdalene, so that he can "refresch" her with "mete and mony, and clothys for þe nyth..." (1651–1653). As Magdalene closes her blessing of the rulers, she announces that the Queen has conceived a child.

Critical in this semiotic reading is that the meaning of these scenes is not to be achieved through language alone. Aligning stage space with characters and literary conventions reveals that these lines have a complex structure dependent upon the visual. Its structure consists of two pairs of dramatic frames embracing a core. The outer frame consists of the King's request for a child and God's favorable response. The inner frame involves Magdalene's prayer for sustenance and the King's favorable response. At the core, luminiscent Magdalene and the two angels appear to the King and Queen at night who wake to conversion.

Magdalene's request for sustenance from Christ in the inner frame and its repetition in the central scene but directed at the King of Marseilles is what creates ambiguity. On the literal level, Christ grants Magdalene's request by having the King give her sustenance. Magdalene, however, then tells the King that in like manner he may serve the poor and God, as an earthly king should do. On another level, this act marks his conversion in the same manner as Magdalene's act of washing and anointing the Lord's feet does. Magdalene does not cleanse and anoint Christ, he cleanses and anoints her with God's grace. Similarly, the King does not relieve Magdalene through his worldly means, she relieves him through her spiritual means.

Transferring this application of the text's semiotic impact to the performative level, it is the juxtaposition of these segments with one another that creates meaning. Assigning to different stage spaces the two framing segments involving the request for a child, the two inner framing segments involving Magdalene's request for sustenance, and the central parade in light, yet making them proceed in this order places weight on the audience's visual linking of the segments in this spectacle.[22] In viewing these scenes, then, it becomes clear through the central light-filled core that these lines work something like a triptych. It is through performance that the playwright creates a staging of what a properly used metaphor might be: words with varying levels of meaning directed towards God's univocal message, salvation. God's words (humans) then become variable, but renewed, metaphors for the same message. The playing space thus represents God's text, as it should be read; the human dynamics occurring within that text work to make sense of God's garden on earth which in its weeded form will become paradise, the type of Eden.

Although a common space can be transformed by actors and staging only to return to the village green once the stage has been dismantled and the audience members have returned to their daily activities, the emptied playing space might nonetheless retain figurative residues. Drama, after all, not only provides edification through entertainment. It also transforms the mundane into the spiritually and aesthetically experienced. The Digby play thus plots out the possibility that the earthly may be redeemed and concomitantly seeks to understand what relation there is between God's words and human words. The semiotic compulsion of the text-centered drama of the middle ages, then, queries relationships between art and life. To put it in the words of Luigi Pirandello's Manager from *Sei personaggi in cerca d'autore (Six Characters in Search of an Author)*:

> Non può stare che un personaggio venga, così, troppo avanti, e sopraffaccia gli altri, invadendo la scena. Bisogna contener tutti in un quadro armonico e rappresentare quel che è rappresentabile! ...ciascuno ha tutta una sua vita dentro e che vorrebbe metterla fuori.
>
> [my translation: One can't let a character walk, like this, too much in the foreground, bullying others, invading the set. Everything must be contained in one harmonious picture and thus represent what is representable! ...everyone has the totality of a life inside—this is what should be transferred to the outside]

NOTES

1. In addition to Ogden's article, see others in the special issue of *Comparative Drama* 8 (Spring 1974), in honor of William L. Smolden.

2. See Corti. I rely heavily on Corti's analysis of how the literary system works, and on its need to rely on conventions. She argues that the ability to read a text against a greater literary context can occur because of literature's viability as a communication system.

3. See Bush, Grantley (a), Twycross, and Grantley (c) and Twycross (b).

4. The play's over 50 characters spanning about 30 years in various locations below, on, and above the earth have led a number of critics to characterize the play as too loose and

unorganized, or as a simple appeal to spectacle. Among them are: Bates: 156, Bennett: 2, Craig: 317, Pollard: 193, Rossiter: 95, Schmidt: 372, and Williams: 166. Other critics have been more appreciative of its strengths, particularly of its symbolism and themes. See, for example, Coletti, Davidson, Jeffrey, Sherb, and Velz.

5. See Brawer who details traits of the resurrction play, all of which can be seen in the Digby play.

6. In contrast to Shakespeare's courtiers, of course, Magdalene is critical to Christ's life. See Brawer on how medieval drama allows for the importance of Mary Magdalene's life in Christ's later life, especially in revealing the miracles after the crucifixion. In the Digby play, Christ appears on stage: at Simon's dinner, to forgive her (614 s.d.–704); at Lazarus' death, to resurrect her brother as well as her faith (846–924, n.b. 891–892); in the *Hortulanus* scene, to resuscitate her faith once again (1055–1095); in the scene in which he praises the Virgin and sets Magdalene a task (1349–1375); in the scene in which he assists her with her task and in the wilderness (1587–1599, 2004–2019); and finally, to bring her into heaven (2074–2081).

7. For the playing space, where movement occurs, in contrast to the platforms, which limit movement, see Bush: 140–145.

8. See Flanigan: 50, who cites Dom Odo Casel on worship as containing consciousness of the past and the future of salvation history in a present moment.

9. See Sherb: 4–9, where he argues Magdalene is herself a *nuntia*, a messenger of God's word, an instance of the logos incarnate.

10. Deely argues that Augustine's *De Doctrina Christiana* is the first extensive treatise on semiotics in western Europe.

11. By the fifteenth century, such teachings of the Church Father (written ten centuries prior to the play) were commonly disseminated as witnessed in the non-literary forms of stained

glass windows which juxtaposed antetypes of the Old Testament with types of the New Testament.

12.　For discussion on Augustine's approach to language, see Colish: 8–81.

13.　Brawer: 96, discusses how the audience to a liturgical play can become actors by participating in the mystery of the service. This principle can be seen to work in the Digby play as well, when for example, the physical actions of the actors are understood emblematically as models of behavior.

14.　As Bush: 151, states: "Man's desire to play God or to appropriate God's language always points to God and the correct use of his language. Inversion but not escape is possible."

15.　To underscore the difference between worldly and spiritual light, fire is always visible under Satan's scaffold (357 s.d.). In addition, he and his associates frequently use fire imagery (e.g., 353, 967), and he has a house set on fire (744 s.d.–747), an act contrasted with one of Magdalene's, whose prayers cause a pagan temple to burn (1561 s.d., cf. 1448). Light imagery is signalled early on as redemptive, when used by Christ or to refer to him (e.g., 175–176, 622–623).

16. On juxtaposition, framing, and the recapitulation of symbols as typical of medieval drama, see Sheingorn.

17.　However, although she falls to pride, arrogance such as that of the blustery rulers is not one of her linguistic characteristics, suggesting that all who turn from Christ are not simply the same.

18. Interestingly, Elam: 11–12, refers to the polysemic character of the theatrical sign functioning as quotation marks. Thus, an object which would not have much significance in daily life acquires heightened significance simply by being placed on the stage, a principle that may also be applied to these banquet scenes.

19.　See Coletti, who argues the importance of banqueting, nourishment, and clothing in the play. She stresses the physical indulgences of the banquet and its symbolic connection to lust.

20. An interesting, worldly parallel to Magdalene's spiritual thirst and hunger is made in the scene involving the shipmaster and his boy, who also desire meat and drink (e.g., 1399, 1403).

21. The narrative playing-out of a convention seems to be a favorite method of the Digby playwright, used, apparently, to revive stale allegories or metaphors. For example, the supernatural rulers—the World, the Flesh, and the Devil—are separated into different locations, with different functions, although their blustery speeches focused on the jealous guarding of power suggest the traditional links among themselves, as well as to the worldly rulers—Tiberius, Herod, and Pilate—through, appropriately, World. Thus, the playwright is not observing codes, nor exactly breaking them, but using them to convey a new message.

22. Similarly, given the generally known episodes of her life, the audience might very well expect Magdalene to fall to the sin of lechery. Indeed, Lechery tempts her from her Castle upon her father's death (440–459), and shortly thereafter, we witness Magdalene in the tavern (470–546). But her gallant here is Curiosity, whom the Bad Angel identifies as Pride, "3a, Pryde, callyd Coriosté, to hure is ful lavdabyll" (550). In other words, the Castle and the Tavern provide worldly spaces that become overcoded to suggest that adherence to any worldly space derives from the sin of pride.

REFERENCES

Baker, Donald C., John L. Murphy, and Louis B. Hall, Jr., eds. 1982. *The Late Medieval Religious Plays of Bodleian MSS Digby 133 and E Museo 160*. Early English Text Society. Oxford: Oxford University Press.

Bates, Katherine Lee. 1926. *The English Religious Drama*. New York: MacMillan.

Beadle, Richard, ed. 1994. *The Cambridge Companion to Medieval English Theatre*. Cambridge: Cambridge University Press.

Bennett, Jacob. 1978. "The *Mary Magdalene* of Bishop's Lynn", *Studies in Philology* 75: 1–9.

Benson, Larry D., gen. ed. 1987, 3rd ed. *The Riverside Chaucer*. Boston: Houghton Mifflin.

Brawer, Robert A. 1974. "The Middle English Resurrection Play and its Dramatic Antecedents." *Comparative Drama* 8: 77–100.

Briscoe, Marianne G. and John C. Coldewey, eds. 1989. *Contexts for Early English Drama*. Bloomington, IN: Indiana University Press.

Bush, Jerome. 1989. "The Resources of *Locus* and *Platea* Staging: The Digby *Mary Madgelene*." *Studies in Philology* 86: 139–145.

Coldewey, John C. 1989. "Some Economic Aspects of the Late Medieval Drama." In Brisco, cited above, 77–101.

Coletti, Theresa. 1979. "The Design of the Digby Play of *Mary Magdalene*." *Studies in Philology* 76: 313–333.

Colish, Marcia L. 1983. *The Mirror of Language: A Study in the Medieval Theory of Knowldege*. Lincoln: University of Nebraska Press.

Corti, Maria. 1978. *An Introduction to Literary Semiotics*. Trans. Margherita Bogat and Allen Mandelbaum. Bloomington IN: Indiana University Press.

Charity, Alan C. 1966. *Events and Their Afterlife: The Dialectics of Christian Typology in the Bible and Dante*. Cambridge: Cambridge University Press.

Craig, Hardin. 1955. *English Religious Drama of the Middle Ages*. Oxford: Clarendon.

Davidson, Clifford. 1972. "The Digby *Mary Magdalene* and the Magdalene Cult of the Middle Ages." *Annuale Medievale* 13: 70–87.

Deely, John. 1982. *Introducing Semiotic: Its History and Doctrine.* Bloomington, IN: Indiana University Press.

Denny, Neville, ed. 1973. *Medieval Drama* London: Edward Arnold.

Elam, Keir. 1988. *The Semiotics of Theatre and Drama.* New Accents. London and New York: Routledge.

Flanigan, C. Clifford. 1974. "The Liturgical Context of the *Quem Queritis* Trope," *Comparative Drama* 8: 45–62.

Gellrich, Jesse M. 1985. *The Idea of the Book in the Middle Ages: Language Theory, Mythology, and Fiction.* Ithaca: Cornell University Press.

Grantley, Darryll. (a) 1983. "Producing Miracles." In Neuss, cited below, 78–91.

———. (b) 1984. "The Source of the Digby *Mary Magdalen.*" *Notes and Queries* 229 n.s. 31: 457–459.

———. (c) 1994. "Saints' Plays." In Beadle, cited above, 270–282.

Jeffrey, David L. 1973. "English Saints' Plays." In Denny, cited above, 69–90.

Kindermann, Heinz. 1980. *Das Theaterpublikum des Mittelalters.* Salzburg: Otto Müller.

Murray, A.T., trans. 1946. Homer, *The Odyssey.* London: William Heinemann.

Neuss, Paula, ed. 1983. *Aspects of Early English Drama.* Cambridge: D. S. Brewer.

Ogden, Dunbar H. 1974. "The Use of Architectural Space in Medieval Music-Drama." *Comparative Drama* 8: 63–76.

Pirandello, Luigi. 1975. *Maschere Nude*, Vol 1. I Classici Contemporanei Italiani: Opere di Luigi Pirandello. Verona: Arnoldo Mondadori.

Pollard, Alfred W. 1895. *English Miracle Plays, Moralities, and Interludes*. Oxford: Clarendon.

Rossiter, A. P. 1950. *English Drama*. London: Hutchinson.

Sheingorn, Pamela. 1989. "The Visual Language of Drama: Principles of Composition." In Briscoe and Coldewey, cited above, 173–191.

Schmidt, K. 1885. "Die Digbyspiele", *Anglia* 8: 371–404.

Sherb, Victor I. 1992. "Worldly and Sacred Messengers in the Digby *Mary Magdalene*." *English Studies* 73: 1–9.

Twycross, Meg. (a) 1988. "Beyond the Picture Theory: Image and Activity in Medieval Drama." *Word & Image* 4: 589–617.

———. (b) 1994. "The Theatricality of Medieval English Plays." in Beadle, cited above, 56–63.

Velz, John M. 1968. "Sovereignity in the Digby *Mary Magdalene*." *Comparative Drama* 2: 32–41.

Williams, Arnold. 1961. *The Drama of Medieval England*. East Lansing, MI: Michigan State University Press.

CHAPTER FIVE

THE CONVERSION OF THE SIGN IN THE TOWNELEY PASSION PLAYS

Mavis G. Fionella

As a part of a project to produce a semiotic reading of the Towneley cycle of mystery plays, I would like to examine the Passion plays from the perspective of Lacanian theory in order to suggest their potential role in the production of Christian subjectivity. Since certain semiotic theories view meaning as a cultural product, they can provide a standpoint outside and apart from the logocentrism that underlies the plays and traditional criticism of them. More important for my purpose, they treat viewers as linguistic subjects of theatrical discourse, giving "due weight to the audience as the ultimate maker of its own meaning" (Elam: 7).

The ideological agency of the plays becomes visible when we find a way to discuss the relation between viewers and their own discourse. Fredric Jameson (Jameson: 30) defines ideology as "a representational structure which allows the individual subject to conceive or imagine his or her lived relationship to transpersonal realities such as the social structure or the collective logic of History." If we assume that viewers are cued to produce some version of Christian sacred history in order to make sense of the plays, their relation to it may be examined by using Lacan's distinction between the positions of subject of the enounced and the subject of the enunciation. Lacan (Lacan: 90) argues that it is "always in the relation between the subject's ego (*moi*) and the "I" (*je*) of his discourse that you must understand the discourse..." His dictum allows us to investigate the relations between viewers and their representations and to argue for the plays' agency in the construction of the Christian subject. Since I will treat viewers as linguistic subjects in this essay, I would like first to offer an hypothesis about the Christian situation of discourse and then to present a reading of the Towneley Passion Plays that illustrates it.

I believe that the plays, like Christian representation in general, set out to rehearse a change in viewers' signifying code and with it, a change in subjectivity. Christian writers on "conversion," such as Paul and Augustine, represented it as a radical transformation in mind and heart that changed the subject's point of view from "sin" to "faith," or "letter" to "spirit," and produced new ideas of world and self (e.g., *Ephesians* 4. 22-4). But conversion to Christian faith involved more than an access to belief in the truth of the gospels or sacred history. Its deepest mechanism operated, I believe, when subjects introjected the code that *produced* gospel and salvation narratives. Members of medieval Christian communities were taught its workings through liturgical readings, homilies and sermons, and Christian art (stained glass, paintings, plays) effectively rehearsed them in the production of its meaning. Reading Christian representation constituted "conversion" by inscribing a change in the signifying code that had powerful implications for subjectivity.

In order to see how such a change might have been effected, let us begin with the hypothesis that Christianity restructured perception of the discursive situation. Benveniste (Benveniste: 225) argues that the primary function of language is to construct the subject. Every speaker becomes a subject by saying (or implying) "ego," which dialectically differentiates it from a "you" or other: "neither of the terms can be conceived of without the other; they are complementary, although according to an 'interior/exterior' opposition, and, at the same time, they are reversible." But the dialectic is not even-handed: "This polarity does not mean either equality or symmetry: 'ego' always has a position of transcendence with regard to *you*." I would like to suggest that Christianity reversed the poles of the dialectic by constructing a perception of a transcendental "Outside" of discourse where the Logos then appeared to be located.

Lacan (Lacan: 174) argues that "the slightest alteration in the relation between man and the signifier, [for example] in the procedures of exegesis, changes the whole course of history by modifying the moorings that anchor his being." The code of Christian typology seems to have been formed dialectically in and by such an alteration. It produced a new narrative from Jewish Scripture and reinterpreted that Scripture in the process to produce a book called the "Old Testament" that could in turn be assimilated to the unfolding story in the New (Kermode: 18, 107). As Auerbach (Auerbach: 52) has shown, Christian figural interpretation severed Jewish Scripture from its "history and national character" and transformed it into a text that prefigured the story of Christ and his role in cosmic events. More importantly, the code claimed historicity for its second-order meanings: as Auerbach (Auerbach: 53-54) says, "promise and fulfillment are real historical events, which have either happened in the incarnation of the Word, or will happen in the second coming... [Typology] differs from most of the allegorical forms known to us by the historicity both of the sign and what it signifies." In other words, figural meanings were not seen to be profected back onto Jewish Scripture from the present of the gospels or exegesis; already contained in the "promises" of the past, they were invisible and inaudible until the Word became flesh and revealed them.

Claiming historicity for meaning whose literality had not yet occurred implies a transcendental "Outside" or externality of discourse where originary Truth resides beyond the scope of time, language and history. In this connection Derrida (Derrida: 14) argues that the very conception of the sign implies divinity: "The sign and divinity have the same place and time of birth. The age of the sign is essentially theological." The reason derives, he says (Derrida: 13), from the division in the concept of the sign into signifier and signified: "linguistic 'science' cannot... hold on to the difference between signifier and signified—the very idea of the sign—without retaining... the reference to a signified able to 'take place' in its intelligibility... . As the face of pure intelligibility, it refers to an absolute logos to which it is immediately united. This absolute logos was an infinite creative subjectivity in medieval theology: the intelligible face of the sign remains turned toward the word and face of God."

In the medieval view, God's immediate, transparent speech articulated material reality and formed the basis of its intelligibility. In consequence, the meaning and being flowed from the Outside, and the sensible, temporal world became a system that, rightly read, signified divine intentionality or Providence. In contrast, for semiotics, it is the differential system of language whose "alpha" and "omega," present "A" and absent "O," model reality and construct subjectivity by producing the first order of signs. From this viewpoint, Christianity mediated meaning and subjectivity by reinterpreting semiosis as evidence of an internal link to Logos. A linguistic subject can see itself seeing itself, through a recurrence of reflexion that makes it both subject and object of its own internal gaze. But if its recognition of language is suppressed, it will be alienated from the "eye" that gazes and will interpret it as if it signified the "I" of an Other. Consequently, what is internal will seem to become external as the subject "sees" itself as the object of the Other's gaze.

By this means, Christianity re-presented the workings of language *in* the subject *to* the subject; it suppressed the position of subject of the enunciation by teaching subjects to reinterpret their perception of the internal workings of language. This glimpse into the discursive process should permit a subject to recognize that meaning is produced by the mechanisms of language. But, if semiosis is a sign of the Logos, production of meaning will be viewed as reception. When the internalized code selects appropriate meanings, subjects will interpret their appearance to consciousness as "insights" that reveal faith's internal eye and ear. In this way, perhaps, the most fundamental level of human knowing, sensory perception, was bound by the Christian code. Subjects' very perception *of* perception is ideologically harnessed when the ability to form sensory images (or signifiers) is seen as evidence on the one hand that the world is a divine sign-system and on the other, that ego shares in an infinite act of creativity.

Christian subjects do not produce meaning but receive it, in faith's access to (culturally defined) logocentric truth: this reformulation is crucial to understanding the agency of the plays. Their performance directs viewers to produce meaning by opposing codes—faith/sin or spirit/letter—which imply opposing ideas about meaning's origin and foundation. Faith's discourse, as we have seen, is full: it derives from and returns to Presence. In contrast, sin's discourse is empty: it appears to be egocentric fantasy "founded" on absence. But these are ideological formations and the plays attempt (at least in one of their effects) to capture viewers in the dual relation of a Christian Imaginary. Geoffrey Hartman (Hartman: 93) has asked if there is "anything comparable to [Lacan's] mirror-stage on the level of language" and suggests that "there is the well-known magical or religious ambition to possess *the* word." Like the sight of the specular body-image in the mirror, the illusion of hermeneutic totality can capture subjects and cause them to identify with their image in the enounced. In this case, the code merely reverses the poles of the Imaginary, causing subjects to relinquish omnipotence to the Other only to have it secretly returned to them by virtue of their access to *the* Truth. If viewers identify ideas of Jewish and Islamic discourse with the code of "sin"—as they are directed to do by the plays—they will merely enter a cultural form of narcissism that is marked by a Christian master-narrative and its claim to hegemony.

In the second part of my essay, I would like to examine the agency of the Passion Plays in the internal "drama" of subjectivity by examining the theoretical relations between viewers and their own discourse.   Towneley prompts viewers to construe a totalizing narrative from theatrical discourse and to make it the object of their desire for a "truth" that promises subjective and social wholeness. This desire leads to capture in the Imaginary, and I believe it is made to operate with special force in the Passion plays. In order to understand how the plays "work," we must look for a moment at Lacan's topology of the subject.

For Lacan, subjectivity is divided and decentered in the alienating structure strung out between the positions of subject of the enounced and subject of the enunciation.   Human beings accede to subjectivity when desire reaches for the image that comes to meet them in the "mirror" of discourse, and they enter the Imaginary by introjecting it ("That's me!"). Ego is only a representation and, for Lacan, it is always an alienating image based on misrecognition that identifies a subject's desire with ego's desire to be seen, and to see itself, in the ideal. Subjects of the enounced, then, identify with their image in discourse and remain blind to the process of its production. In contrast, the subject of the enunciation (or signifier) is the "I/eye" of the unconscious, and its mechanisms are linguistic. It moves via the two great axes by which language produces meaning, the paradigmatic and syntagmatic chains, which Lacan likens to the mechanisms of metaphor and metonymy. *Ecrits*'s discontinuous discourse is intended to alert readers to their (uncomfortable) position as subject of and to the signifier. But as we have seen, Christianity divided this reflexion, blinding subjects to the internal workings of language by interpreting them as signs of divine Truth.

A macro-segmentation of the plays shows that viewers are led by this shift to reconstruct a chain of signifiers, but to make it the object of their desire as if it were "given" by the plays. The signifiers are metonyms by virtue of their selection from Jewish Scripture; together they generate the story of Christ that, in turn, rationalizes their metonymic linkage. As viewers reproduce the chain, it tells them how to generate the story of Christ that, in turn, rationalizes their metonymic linkage. As viewers reproduce the chain, it tells them how to generate the story. If "Jesus of Nazareth" is "Christ," a series of signifiers is connoted—Son of God, Lamb of God, Savior, Heavenly King—which will appear progressively to be literalized in the plays. As viewers' narrative is reified, desire is moved metonymically along the syntagmatic chain until it accedes to a position in which viewers may "see" themselves, like Magdalen, in an image of transcendental ego. For Lacan, however, desire is a response to lack. Subjectivity is not founded on presence, but alienated across a gap in signification, a lack-of-being symbolized by the bar in the Saussurian algorithm (S/s). As Lemaire (Lemaire: 164) explains, "Hence the metonymic course of desire, forever insatiable since it refers back to the ineffable, to the unconscious desire [for wholeness] and the absolute lack it conceals." From this standpoint, I believe that the Passion plays amplify and direct viewers' desire by bringing them into contact with this moment of absolute lack.

By causing viewers to supply an idea of Jesus's subjectivity, the plays make them "forget" they are watching a theatrical production and respond as if "he possessed independent reality." If Christianity and Lacan (Lacan: 24) agree on any one idea, it seems to be "the irreducible character of the narcissistic structure." Lacan (Lacan: 19) identifies entry into the Imaginary with the source of narcissistic aggressivity. Identification with the specular image awakens the subject's "desire for the object of the other's desire: here the primordial coming together (*concours*) is precipitated into aggressive competitiveness (*concurrence*), from which develops the triad of others, the ego and the object... ." Viewers' relation to the theatrical frame of the Passion reactivates this structure, causing its transference to their narrative.

The Conspiracy, The Scourging and *The Crucifixion* repeatedly cast viewers into the virtual role of Pilate's subjects when he calls for silence and threatens them, ranting and brandishing his sword. Since viewers understand his negative role in advance, the act of frame-breaking may alienate them sufficiently to produce two effects. While they probably reject their implied position within the dramatic world, since he is explicitly subjected to Pilate's power. Their subsequent opposition to the antagonists identifies Jesus's role as the object of desire for each group, the site where each group will seek to constitute ego. In this way, the Passion structures the representational field according to the either/or polarity of narcissistic rivalry, pitting viewers against antagonists in a competition for ascendency as each group tries to secure its interpretation of Jesus's significance.

But we must remember, even if viewers do not, that they construe the utterances of *actors*, not characters. As Serpieri (Serpieri: 167–168) insists, *viewers* constitute the personae and events that actors illustrate through speech and gesture in their given theatrical roles. If this is the case, it follows that the Passion necessarily structures viewers as unwitting rivals to themselves. As subjects *of* the whole theatrical discourse, they are subject *to* both codes, "letter" and "spirit," and they become the field on which the two systems do battle. During the Passion, the two codes work dialectically in and through viewers to construct a clash of opposing implications. In consequence, although they construe the whole discourse, viewers are encouraged to alienate aggressivity in tyrants and tortores, and to institute "Jesus" as immanent subject, situating desire in the reflection that returns to them from him. In general, the Passion leads them to behave like the child in the "Fort/Da" game who institutes the sign and banishes it, in order to bring it back.

The position of subject of the enunciation is suppressed when viewers come to see Jesus as a subject in the dual relation of the Imaginary. Lacan (Lacan: 13, 15) argues that the transference cannot be effected unless the other represents "an ideal of impassibility" or "the pure mirror of an unruffled surface." The most notable dramatic feature of the Passion's central role is precisely its odd impassibility. Jesus seldom speaks, and he does not cry out or struggle against his tormentors—indeed, in *The Crucifixion*, he apparently even positions himself on the cross. At the same time, while antagonists mock and strike him, they seem blind to thoughts of his consciousness of suffering. Since he is represented as object within the dramatic world, his missing role of subject is ostended by implication to viewers who must fill in the blank, so to speak, by supplying an idea of self-consciousness.

The Buffeting effaces their work by a deixis that points to an idea of subjectivity but refuses to formulate it, forcing viewers unwittingly to complete the conceptual act. *The Buffeting* is one of the Master's plays and he employs a technique, notable also in

The Second Shepherds' Play, that uses one dramatic agent in particular to manipulate audience response—in this case, the role of First Tortor. At the beginning of the play, First Tortor attempts to describe a perception of Jesus's face: "Fayn wold he wynk,/ Els falys his countenance; I say as I thynk" (see England for edition: 229, ll. 37–38). Later, he tries to construe expression: "He is sowre lottyn:/ Ther is somwhat forgottyn!/ I shall thryny out the rottyn/ Be we have all talkyd" (232, ll. 123–126). The frustrated outburst makes viewers' discourse founder on a blank that foregrounds their own idea of Jesus's subjectivity but makes it seem "given" in the play. In order to conclude that First Tortor cannot or will not conceptualize Jesus as subject, viewers must first produce the idea themselves. Since they know that First Tortor is one of sin's representatives, they will interpret his discursive omission—which they unwittingly fill in—as a moral failure to see what is *there*, making Jesus's subjectivity appear to be "present," to himself and to them, independent of their own activity.

Furthermore, semiotics can explain how an illusion of theatrical presence might come to signify a metaphysical concept. Eco (Eco: 110) argues that when something is dramatically ostended, picked up and shown, it is derealized as a particular and signifies the class of which it is a member. Jesus speaks reflexively once in *The Buffeting* and once in *The Scourging* to identify himself as the Son of God. If Jesus's subjectivity seems "present" to viewers through a foregrounding of their own conception, the connotation "Son of God" will direct them to interpret it as "Christ," the immanent eye and voice of Presence.

But sin's power appears to prevail in the Passion and for the duration of these plays viewers function as the nexus of a conflict which makes them signify against themselves. The whole force of the letter's discourse—which viewers produce—is pitted against their own production of the signifier "Christ" and the metonymic system it generates. For example, in order to construe the antagonists' discourse, they must reinterpret Jesus as a rival and his speech as a false claim to political kingship. In *The Buffeting* Caiaphas "names" Jesus "king copyn in oure game" (233, ll. 165–166), and the tortores set him up for Hot Cockles like a mock-king. They crown him with thorns in *The Scourging* and in *The Crucifixion*, viewers must interpret the mounting of Jesus on the cross through an extended metaphor of the horsing of a king for tournament sport.   If irony and double meaning result, it is because viewers project the connotation "heavenly king." If so, they respond once again to their own foregrounded conception, concluding that antagonists are blind to a truth that is there, revealed in the presence of "Christ."

But the letter's hegemony increasingly forces viewers to act out its implications in their discourse.   Animals lack ego or symbolic identity. In Ernest Becker's words (Becker: 26), "If they pause at all, it is only a physical pause; inside they are anonymous, and even their faces have no name."   When the tortores of *The Buffeting* and *The Scourging* lead and drive a bound and silent Jesus—probably among members of the audience— viewers must interpret him through the theatrical metaphor of a work animal, annuling their idea of his subjectivity.   *The Crucifixion* intensifies the effect, amplifying anxiety. It foregrounds discussion of the frustrations of crucifying a body and of the palpable effects upon it of such actions as dropping the cross into the mortise. Viewers must construe Jesus from the viewpoint of the tortores who impute an idea of pain to his body and interpret it as a sign of their effectiveness. In their eyes Jesus is anonymous inside and, even if viewers dissociate the discourse, its assumptions are unconsciously inscribed: "body" is ego's mirror or intractable "stuff"; the signifier is empty.

The internal drama that viewers act out while witnessing the Passion is based on the presence or absence of the signifier, "Christ." But, as we have seen, viewers produce this signifier and project it into the plays; they also unwittingly take it away.   The plays precipitate the narcissistic crisis by making them momentarily speechless, unable to signify.   At this point we should pause to remember that viewers are watching actors who employ dialogue, gesture and props to simulate a crucifixion. Perhaps for the sake of illusion, they have loosely tied "Jesus's" wrists to the crossbars but secured his feet on a footrest so the performer will not fall when they raise the cross. Viewers' belief is directed to an objectified image; if they are blind to their position in the enunciation, they will view "Jesus" as if he were a subject in reality. Consequently, they will forget they are viewing a play and enter into the dual relation of the Christian Imaginary.

Since they have acted as subjects of both systems, spirit and letter, in the moment when Jesus speaks from the cross one code sees the other working *in* viewers, dividing them into the subject/object of their own internal gaze. The dual relation makes the linguistic "I/eye" or code of the spirit seem to speak with the Other's voice and glance with his eye, subjecting viewers to guilt for their part in the letter's discourse. Since viewers stand at the theatrical crucifixion scene, they are cast into a virtual role when Jesus addresses "you pepyll that passe me be" (265, l. 233) and directs them to look at his bloody body and to imagine the suffering they have caused. "My folk, what have I done to the,/ That thou all thus shall tormente me?/ Thy syn by I full sore./ what have I grevyd the? answere me,/ That thou thus nalys me to a tre,/ And all for thyn erroure" (265, ll. 244–249). When he speaks, as if to them, they "see" a subject who knows the purpose of his denial. If they identify with their image in the enounced, they will see their guilt reflected in his knowledge. In other words, they will see themselves seeing themselves as subjects of the letter who have dismembered their object through acts of representation.

And so, for a moment at least, they cannot answer because they have lost the power to signify. When "erroure" is mirrored in the Other's gaze, ego falls in the subject's eyes and guilt revokes the power to bring it back. Subjectivity is cut off, is absent to itself, as the void in signification opens. Lacan (Lemaire: 72) says that "The drama of the subject in the verb [verbum or copula] is that he faces the test of his lack of being. It is because it fends off this moment of lack that an image moves into position to support the whole worth of desire: profection, a function of the Imaginary." Having taken it away, the words from the cross allow viewers to remobilize the signifier that returns the syntagmatic chain in which ego desires to be constituted. Through Jesus's forgiving words, viewers regain their relation with an idea of "Christ" by generating the metonym "Lamb of God." Operating at the interface of the two codes, the signifier "Lamb of God" turns the intelligible face of the sign toward God. It is the object of profected guilt who, by becoming a subject, gives back the efficacy of its suffering so that viewers may see themselves reflected in it (for me!). In the perception of modern linguistic theory, the signifier *is* empty or arbitrary; and subjectivity is contingent upon language. The passion plays represent this perception ideologically in order to secure the logocentric code. The intersection of the codes of letter and spirit in *The Crucifixion* takes semiosis away in order to give it back, so that viewers will introject the code that structures Christian subjectivity and take their places in the social "Body" of Christ.

NOTE

1. Kermode: 18 comments that the joining in the late second century of the Old Testament to the New "was of a kind that permitted Christian interpreters to assume that the more obvious senses of the Old Testament, including its historical meaning, were of small or no importance, were dangerous illusions, even. The Old Testament made sense only insofar as it prefigured Christianity."

REFERENCES

Auerbach, Erich. 1959. "Figura." In *Scenes from the Drama of European Literature*. New York: Meridian Books, 11–76.

Becker, Ernest. 1973. *The Denial of Death*. New York: Free Press.

Benveniste, Emile. 1966. *Problèmes de linguistique generale*. Editions Gallimard. Page references in the present article are to the English trans. by Mary Elizabeth Meek. 1971. *Problems in General Linguistic*. Florida: University of Miami Press.

Derrida, Jacques. 1967. *De la Grammatologie*. Les Editions de Minuit. Page references in the present article are to the English trans. by Gayatri Chakravorty Spivak. 1976. *Of Grammatology*. Baltimore: Johns Hopkins University Press.

Eco, Umberto. 1977. "The Semiotics of Theatrical Performance," *Drama Review* 21: 107–117.

Elam, Keir. 1980. *The Semiotics of Theatre and Drama*. New York: Methuen.

England, George and Alfred W. Pollard, eds. 1897. *The Towneley Plays*. Early English Text Society. London: Kegan, Paul, Trench, Trubner.

Hartman, Geoffrey H. 1978. "Psychoanalysis: The French Connection." In *Psychoanalysis and the Question of the Text*. ed. Geoffrey H. Hartman. Baltimore: Johns Hopkins University Press, 86–113.

Jameson, Fredric. 1981. *The Political Unconscious*. Ithaca: Cornell University Press.

Kermode, Frank. 1979. *The Genesis of Secrecy*. Cambridge, MA: Harvard University Press.

Lacan, Jacques. 1966. *Ecrits*. Editions du Seuil. Page references in the present article are to the English trans. by Alan Sheridan. 1977. *Ecrits: A Selection*. New York: W.W. Norton.

Lemaire, Anika. 1977, 2nd ed, rev. *Jacques Lacan*. Trans. David Macey. Boston: Routledge & Kegan Paul.

Serpieri, Alessandro. 1981. "Toward a Segmentation of the Dramatic Text." *Poetics Today* 2: 163–200.

CHAPTER SIX

THE MODES OF THE OLD ENGLISH METRICAL CHARMS—THE TEXTS OF MAGIC

Lois Bragg

There are eighty-six Anglo-Saxon charms extant, chiefly in two manuscripts, the tenth-century *Læceboc* and the eleventh-century *Lacnunga*, although many appear in other manuscripts as well, often in the margins.[1] Of these charms, some are wholly in Latin, some in what appears to be gibberish,[2] many in Old English prose, and twelve in Old English verse, either in whole or in part. The twelve metrical charms have attracted a great deal of scholarly attention in recent years, chiefly from students of literature rather than from anthropologists. Indeed, several of the metrical charms have considerable literary merit despite their often irregular prosody. In the words of Eliza Butler, extant texts of ritual magic

> ...show evidence of creative instincts, poetical imagination and feeling for beauty and drama, in however rude and embryonic a state. This is what makes the study of ritual magic still interesting today; for the aesthetic element, inherent in the nature of the ceremonial, can be detected struggling to emerge. (4)

In addition, because these pieces function both as literature and as magic, they provide an opportunity to investigate some of the claims made by structuralists of several disciplines and by semioticians that would link art, myth, ritual, magic, popular culture—indeed, all human endeavor—into a complete system. This is my purpose here: to investigate the extent to which the literary aspects of the metrical charms are linked to their magical methods.

The charms as we have them can be thought of as scripts, for they comprise not only the incantation or spell, which is usually in verse, but, in most cases, the prose directions for action to accompany the spell. Some of the metrical charms comprise spells alone, but none comprises directions alone: since the directions are never given in verse, metrical charms necessarily include a spell. By *charm*, then, I mean the entire script, both spell and directions for action, when they appear. Anthropologists are divided over the question of which of these two components is primary.[3] However, John L. Austin's studies of speech acts indicates that the distinction between spell and act is not as sharp as we once thought, for to give an order which must inevitably be followed (or so the magician supposes) is to act. In fact, even "stating something is performing an act just as much as is giving an order"(Austin: 251).[4] The spell sections of the Old English metrical charms include many instances of commands, but they also include a great deal of simple statement in the form of analogies, metaphors, and narratives.[5] The nature of the connection between this literary component—the verse analogies, metaphors and narratives—and the magical component—or, more precisely, between the literary aspect and the magical aspect—is the subject of my investigation.

Before proceeding, it is necessary further to define the spell by distinguishing it from the prayer. The distinction between the prayer and the spell is often denied, yet most anthropologists and linguists, following Frazer, do distinguish them thus: the prayer supplicates a spirit or deity to bring about an act in accordance with the wisher expressed in the prayer, while the spell "assumes that in nature one event [the desired effect] follows another [the magical act] necessarily and invariable without the intervention of any spiritual or personal agency" (Frazer: 56). Roman Jakobson uses the terms "supplicatory" and "exhortative": the distinction rests in whether the speaker is subordinate to the addressee, as in prayer, or the addressee is subordinate to speaker, as in the spell. In short, prayers ask; spells act. Of course, as is obvious to anyone who has ever looked at magical charms, the religious element or mode appears frequently, and often it is impossible to separate the religious from the magical, the supplication from the exhortation. Nevertheless, the distinction is useful and will be observed in this study.[6]

Frazer was the first to distinguish two modes of sympathetic magic: homeopathic magic and contagious magic.

> If we analyze the principles of thought upon which magic is based, they will probably be found to resolve themselves into two: first, that like produces like, or that an effect resembles its cause; and second, that things which have once been in contact with each other continue to act on each other at a distance after the physical contact has been severed. The former principle may

be called the Law of Similarity, the latter the Law of Contact or Contagion. From the first of the principles, namely the Law of Similarity, the magician infers that he can produce any effect he desires merely by imitating it; from the second he infers that whatever he does to a material object will affect equally the person with whom the object was once in contact, whether it formed part of his body or not. Charms based on the Law of Similarity may be called Homeopathic or Imitative Magic. Charms based on the Law of Contact or Contagion may be called Contagious Magic. (12–13)

Jakobson, in "Two Aspects of Language and Two Types of Aphasic Disturbances," adopted Frazer's binary model of magic into a comprehensive model of language. According to his model, language functions by linking ideas either through their similarity or their contiguity. The evidence he gives for these two modes of language range from the study of aphasiacs through the work of Frazer to the study of figurative language in literature. Thus the principle underlying the similarity disorder in aphasiacs corresponds to homeopathic magic and to the metaphor in literature, while the principle underlying the contiguity disorder in aphasiacs corresponds to contagious magic and to the metonym in literature. Jakobson calls these two modes the metaphoric and the metonymic, taking the designations from literary study because it is in literature that these two modes "find their most condensed expression" [Jakobson (b): 90].

The distinction between these two modes of language had already been established by Ferdinand de Saussure in his *Course in General Linguistics*. Saussure recognized two axes in language function. One, the synchronic axis, involves relationships among coexisting members in a system. The other axis, the diachronic axis, involves elements that may be substituted for one another but do not form a system. The diachronic axis is thus paradigmatic and involves selection rather than combination. Jakobson's two modes thus corresponds to Saussure's two axes: the axis of combination corresponds to the metonymic mode. The terminology given here is staggering and has yet to be regularized, so it is useful to list these terms in a table:

metaphoric	*metonymic*
homeopathic magic	contagious magic
similarity disorder in aphasia	contiguity disorder in aphasia
metaphor	metonymy (including synecdoche)
diachronic axis	synchronic axis
paradigm	syntagm
selection	combination

Despite the difficulty of the terms, however, the concept of the binary model is really quite simple. To illustrate: in composing a song, one chooses a single tone from among the twelve tones of our scale and juxtaposes in with a second tone, chosen likewise from among the twelve possible tones, and so on. The set of the twelve possible tones is Saussure's diachronic axis (or paradigmatic axis, or axis of selection), and when we choose one of these notes we are operating in the metaphoric mode (the mode of combination). Another common example is in assembling an outfit of clothing. We choose sneakers from among a set of like articles that includes boots, pumps, sandals, and so on, thus operating in the axis of selection, and add to the sneakers a pair of jeans and a tee shirt, thus operating in the axis of combination. The collection of footwear we have in our closets is a paradigmatic set, while the complete outfit of sneakers, jeans, and tee shirt is a syntagmatic system. As for figurative language, the literary metaphor involves selecting from a group of like concepts, such as old age, evening and autumn. When a writer uses autumn to stand for old age, for example, he or she is working in the selection axis which involves perception of similarity. Autumn and old age are, of course, not at all similar in themselves, but they stand in similar relationships to larger concepts. To use John Austin's terms, A:B::X:Y, where old age is to the human life cycle as autumn is to the year's cycle (Austin: 71–72). The literary metonym, on the other hand, including synecdoche, which is a kind of metonymy, involves combining concepts in contiguity, as when gray hair or a cone stands for old age. In using a metonym such as gray hair, the writer is operating in the combination axis, which depends upon perception of contiguity: gray hair accompanies old age. Thus metaphor and metonymy operate according to opposite principles: gray hair is in contiguity with old age but is not similar to it, while autumn is similar to old age, but does not occur in contiguity with it.

The binary model of language has been remarkably productive not only in linguistics but in anthropology, Levi-Strauss being the major figure here,[7] and in literary studies. David Lodge, in *The Modes of Modern Writing*, presents the most thorough application of this model to literary studies. Lodge's purpose is to investigate the differences between the two schools of the twentieth-century novel: the realistic and the modernist. In the process of this investigation, he came upon Jakobson's "Two Aspects of Language," which he found to be "impressive evidence for the theory that metaphor and metonymy are "polar opposites" (Lodge: 77). Jakobson's binary model proved to be the key to Lodge's further studies (Lodge: x). The beauty of the binary system is that it is "capable of being applied to data at different levels of generality" (Lodge: 80): thus, it is useful not only in discussing figures of speech, but in discussing entire novels as well. He concluded that the two schools of the twentieth-century novel represent the two modes of language, the realistic novel representing the metonymic mode and the modernist novel representing the metaphoric mode. Looking at the distinction more widely, Lodge finds that poetry is most representative of the metaphoric mode, because it is based on "relationships of the metaphoric mode, because it is based on "relationships of similarity", while prose of all kinds is chiefly metonymic, because, to quote Jakobson, it is "forwarded essentially by contiguity" [Lodge: 88, Jakobson (b): 96]. Indeed, "at the highest level of generality at which we can apply the metaphor/metonymy distinction, literature itself is metaphoric and nonliterature metonymic" (Lodge: 109). Thus we can see that although the modes themselves are "polar opposites," the binary model is a continuum along which we can place any text. For example, the novels of Theodore Dreiser would be closer to the metonymic pole than those of Faulkner, but not as close as non-literary discourse. Likewise, Joyces' *Portrait of the Artist as a Young Man* would be placed close to Faulkner's novels but *Ulysses* would be closer to the metaphoric pole and *Finnegan's Wake* closer still. At this point we may add to our list:

metaphor	metonymy
the selection of a tone	the combination of tones in melody
the selecion of a pair of shoes	the combination of clothing in an outfit
"autumn" for "old age"	"gray hair" for "old age"
modernist novels	realistic novels
Finnegan's Wake	*An American Tragedy*
poetry	prose
literature	non-literary discourse

Having thus schematically outlined the binary model and suggested that it has very much to do both with magic and with literature, we are now prepared to look more closely at the model by incorporating the work of C. S. Peirce. Peirce distinguished three kinds of signs: the icon, which is similar to the tenor; the index, which is associated with the tenor through contiguity; and the symbol, which is purely conventional (104–115). As for the first two kinds of signs, it is obvious that the icon falls under the metaphoric mode and the index under the metonymic mode. For example, taking the tenor "fire," smoke would be an effective index. Smoke stands for fire, and can substitute for it, but it is an index, and thus metonymic, because its ability to stand for fire depends solely on the fact that it is found in physical contiguity with fire. On the other hand, an icon for fire might be the orange light bulb that one sometimes finds in certain suburban fireplaces and department store windows. Orange light bulbs are not found in contiguity with fire—where one has fire one has no need for an orange light bulb—and they are not from the same realm of experience, for fire is a natural phenonmenon while orange light bulbs are technological artifacts. An orange light bulb can stand for fire only because tenor and vehicle are similar in one respect: they both put out light of the same. Taking this example, we see that in the metonymic mode, the tenor is not only in the same order of existence as the vehicle, as are fire and smoke, but is also actually present: "Where there's smoke there's fire." In the metaphoric mode, on the other hand, the tenor and vehicle are not only from different orders of experience, but the presence of the vehicle, the orange light bulb, tells us that the tenor, fire, is not present.

The concept of whether the tenor and vehicle belong to the same or different orders of experience is especially helpful in discussions of analogy, especially simile. As Lodge points out, the word *like* is ambiguous, for it may convey a genuine simile, which is a kind of metaphor and which belongs to the metaphoric mode because it shows similarity between things that are essentially dissimilar. On the other hand, *like* may indicate a metonym, in that it may show not similarity but rather representation, a part for the whole. (Lodge: 112) In other words, if the tenor and vehicle of the analogy belong to the same order, their relationship is one of contiguity, not similarity. To give an example: "like a cherry" is metaphoric in the sentence "His nose is like a cherry" because noses and cherries belong to different sets, but it is metonymic in the sentence "A plum is like a cherry" because plums and cherries do belong to the same set, it this case the genus *Prunus*. To add to out list:

metaphoric	*metonymic*
icon	index
light bulb stands for fire	smoke stands for fire
metaphoric simile	metonymic analogy
"nose like a cherry"	"plum like a cherry"

Roger Browne, in his important essay on "The Typology of Literary Signs," thus rightly concludes that metonymy involves not only physical contiguity but also "any coexistence between two things in the same spatio-temporal continuum" (Browne: 11). This is why metonymy is not as strikingly "literary" as metaphor, or in contrast to the metaphor, which, if it is fresh, will surprise the reader, metonymy seems "logical and inevitable" (Browne: 14). Metonymy does not require the imaginative leap that metaphor requires, for rather than leaping from one context (such as noses) to another (such as fruit), metonymy remains in the same context (one fruit for another).

The amount of distance between the vehicle and the tenor in the metaphor is very important: the greater the distance, or the more incongruous the realms, the more powerful the metaphor, but also the more disturbing to the reader's sense of reality (Lodge: 112). Brian Wicker, in *The Story-Shaped World*, develops the idea further. The distance between the tenor and the vehicle of a metaphor is great enough that comprehension of the metaphor requires denial of its literal truth (Wicker: 26), a denial that is *not* required by the metonym. Further, Wicker states that "metaphor is not just a way of describing things, but is a way of *experiencing* them" (Wicker: 11). Metaphor, then, is intrinsically connected with a "metaphysical world-view" (Wicker: 4). An example taken from Fred G. See's essay on William Dean Howells will illustrate this point. In investigating the realistic fiction of Howells, See contrasts the metonymic language of realistic fiction with the metaphoric language of what he calls "romantic fiction."

> Romantic fiction…uses symbolic language [i.e., metaphor] to transform the evidence of the senses into the signs of a non-temporal and supernatural experience. What takes place is a transfiguration of the reader's imagination, in which the events of history become the manifestation of a divine will. The process of romantic language is thus a transcendent one. It elevates the perception and influences consciousness to read the world as the vast metaphor of a sacred design. (381)

See's remarks on the romantic novel are precisely applicable to magical charms. Metaphoric language and homeopathic magic involve transfiguration from the context at hand to a larger, metaphysical context, and transcendence from the temporal sphere to the non-temporal. While metonymic magic seems logical in its attempt to effect a result by shuffling terms and objects which belong to the same order of experience, metaphoric magic leaps the boundary of the temporal experience and conjures up the supernatural design of the universe. To complete our list:

metaphoric	*metonymic*
distance between tenor and vehicle	no distance between tenor and vehicle
a leap between two contexts	the same context
requires denial of literal truth	can be understood literally
implies a metaphysical world-view	implies a physical world-view

In the Old English metrical charms, which are both magical and literary, we expect that those charms functioning in the metonymic mode, by contagious magic and metonymic language, will appear logical and inevitable, realistic and non-literary, while those functioning in the metaphoric mode, by homeopathic magic and metaphoric language, will appear startling and will transform the mundane context into the mystic—and the literary. This is, in fact, exactly what we find.

Metonymic Charms

Most of the Old English metrical charms are metonymic or have major metonymic sections. This is not surprising, for the literature as a whole is chiefly metonymic. Even the Old English lyric poetry is more metonymic than that of the later Middle Ages and beyond. Rather than attempt to discuss the metonymic mode wherever it appears, I have selected several charms that are most typical and interesting.

"For a Swarm of Bees" is a metonymic charm that relies chiefly on contagious magic. I give the charm in full:

> Against a swarm of bees, take earth, throw it down
>   with your right hand under your right foot, and say:
>   I seized it under foot, I found it.
>   Lo, the earth has the power against all kinds of creatures
>   and against enmity and against jealousy
>   and against the great tongue of man.
> And throw earth over them when they swarm and say:
>   Sit victory-women, sink to earth.
>   Never fly wild to the woods.
>   Be as mindful of my good
>   as each man is of his food and homeland.

The handful of earth is a synecdoche for the earth itself. The earth has power over all things, and the charmer has power over the earth, metonymically represented by the handful cast under her or his right foot. When that handful is thrown over the swarm, the power of the earth, subject to the power of the charmer, is put into physical contact with the swarm, and the desired result is effected: they settle on the beekeeper's property. This charm seems quite logical. It is likely that casting a handful of earth over a swarm would indeed break their flight. The final two lines employ an analogy: "Be as mindful of my good as every man is of his food and homeland." Here, the vehicle, "every man," and the tenor, the bees, are not far removed. Honey is not only the Anglo-Saxons' food, but the bees' food as well. And, both beekeeper and bees have been sharing the same homeland. To make sure that they continue to share the same homeland—that the bees remain on he beekeeper's property—is the object of the charm.

A more sophisticated metonymic charm is found in "For Unfruitful Land." This charm is usually recognized as a two-part charm although sometimes treated as an organic whole. However, it seems obvious that it is actually a conflation of two distinct charms, the first (1–44) for pasture land, and the second (45–82) for cultivated land. Clearly, these two charms could not have been used in conjunction on the same field, although both may have formed part of a spring ritual.[8] The first of these, which I designate "For Unfruitful Land A," uses contagious magic and metonymic language in an attempt to bring the sun into fruitful contact with the pasture. In fact, this charm seems to be a remnant of pagan sun worship, overlayed with a thin Christian veneer.

To summarize: During the night, the magician is to cut four pieces of sod, one from each side of the pasture, and to dress the underside of these sods with a mixture of oil, honey, yeast, milk from each that grazes in that pasture, a piece of each kind of tree and plant (with two explicit exceptions) that grows in the pasture, and holy water. The sods are then to be taken to a church, placed with their top sides toward the altar, returned to the field during daylight, and replaced in their holes, into which holes have been placed four crosses of aspen wood, each inscribed with the name of one of the four evangelists. The magician is then to face the east, recite a prayer, turn three times in the direction of the sun's path, stretch him- or herself out on the ground, and recite more prayers with out-stretched arms, this time, Christian formulæ whose texts are not included.

The making of crosses pervades this poem. In addition to the aspen wood crosses, there is the removal of the four sods, which action forms a cross over the entire pasture, and the stretching out of the magician's arms, which forms a cross of her or his body. The cross is, of course, a familiar symbol for the sun in Germanic paganism,[9] and it seems that the sun's help, rather than Christ's is the object of the entire charm. First, the sods are removed during the night, when the sun is not present, and returned during the day, in the sun's presence. The prayers are spoken facing the direction of the sun's rising, and the magician moves in the direction of the sun's path. All of these actions, the making of crosses, orientation, and extending the arms, are metonymic: their purpose is to bring the sun into contact with the charmer and the pasture. This contagious magic does involve some metaphoric aspects, such as the iconic turning in the direction of the sun's path and the conventional symbol for the sun. Daylight, however, is an index for the sun, and thus metonymic. Other aspects of the charms are metonymic as well. The four sods themselves synecdochically represent the entire pasture. The oil, honey, yeast, holy water, and milk to be poured on the undersides of the sods are metonymic: the oil, honey, yeast, and milk are indices of fertility, while the holy water is probably a Christian substitute for dew,[10] which is likewise an index of fertility. The directions for the other ingredients in this mixture, the pieces of each kind of tree and plant growing in the pasture, specifically excludes hardwood trees and burdock. The exclusion of hardwoods may indicate religious reverence (Rosenberg: 432), but it seems more likely that the charm intends to include evergreens only (Magoun), which are common indices of fertility (and as such have survived in modern Christmas rituals). The reason for the exclusion of the burdock is unclear: perhaps its perpetuation was not desired.

The only section of this charm to be in verse is the prayer said facing the east. This section can be called a prayer in that it asks, rather than exhorts, but what it asks "the guardian of the heavenly kingdom" and St. Mary for is not divine intervention but rather the ability effectively to utter the charm and to bring about fertility "through strong thought." Thus, despite many Christian elements, the charm is essentially magical. And, as a metonymic charm, it is chiefly in prose. There is nothing literary about the prayer other than its verse form.

Another metonymic charm, which appears in two versions, both titled "For Loss of Cattle," makes pervasive use of the cross symbol. This charm begins with directions to the owner of the lost cattle to speak these lines before saying anything else:

> Bethlehem is the name of the town in which Christ was born,
> it is famous throughout all the earth;
> thus may this deed become famous among mankind
> through the holy Cross of Christ.

The owner is then to face the east and say three times "Crux Christi ab oriente reducao," then the west, south, and north, each time repeating the formula three times. While facing the last direction, these words are added:

> Crux Christi abscondita est et inventa est. The Jews
> crucified Christ, did the worst of deeds, they were not
> able to conceal the savior. Thus may this deed in no
> way be hidden through the holy Cross of Christ. Amen.

In this charm, the formation of a cross by facing successively each of the four directions seems thoroughly Christian. Storms sees this ritualistic action as a remnant of sun worship: the cattle certainly cannot be hidden from the sun, so the charmer forms the symbol of the sun to bring it into the search (214). Thomas D. Hill offers a Christian rationale for the action, suggesting that the facing of the four directions describes the "cosmological Cross" which imposes order on space. The cross formed by this action will thus restore order out of the disorder created by the theft of the cattle. It is not unlikely that both the sun and the cosmological Cross have had a hand in the creation of this charm and several other Germanic charms that employ similar actions. However, commentators on this charm miss the obvious in failing to observe that when one has lost one's cattle, it is logical to look around for them, which is exactly what the directions have one do, albeit in a highly stylized form.

This charm is highly logical, and, except for the symbol of the cross and its iconic representation in the actions of the charmer, wholly metonymic. Nigel F. Barley points out the element of contagious magic in the first lines: "before you say anything else..."; that is, it is important not to make contact with any other concepts but to keep oneself in linguistic and physical contact with the cattle (71). Bringing the sun or the Cross into the cattle pasture is metonymic as well, as is the use of analogies. A property of the Cross is self-manifestation, the power to restore itself to its rightful place as a central object of Christianity. Thus, the Cross is an index of the concept "to become manifest," and the analogy is metonymic: to say "may the cattle be like the Cross" is to say "may the cattle and the Cross belong to the same set of things that were lost and will necessarily be found." The reference to Bethlehem widens the set to "all well-known things": Bethlehem, the Cross, and the theft of cattle are all indices of "fame."

The other metrical cattle charm, titled "For Theft of Cattle," begins with similar metonymic analogies.

> May nothing that I own be stolen or hidden anymore than
> Herod was able to steal or hide our Lord. I thought of
> St. Helen and I thought of Christ hanging on the Cross;
> thus I think of finding the cattle...

Here the analogies are a little more explicit. The infant Christ, the Cross, and the cattle all belong to the set of things that cannot successfully be stolen and hidden. Herod and the cattle thief belong to the set of unsuccessful thieves. St. Helen and the charmer belong to the set of people who discover stolen objects.

Both of these cattle charms thus rely on metonymic analogies. The vehicles—Bethlehem, the Cross, Herod, St. Helen—seem at first sight to be fairly far removed from the tenor, the theft of cattle. They are certainly far removed in space and time, and the modern reader would say that the vehicles belong to a mythical realm while the tenor belongs to the realm of mundane husbandry. However, a closer look reveals that the charm operates by placing the theft of the cattle into logical sets that include what were to the Anglo-Saxons other historical events. The analogies function by placing the charmer, the cattle, and the thief into sets of things or concepts which the charmer desires. The charmer wishes to be like St. Helen, for example, to be another representative of "people who find and restore things."

"The Nine Herbs Charm" provides other examples of metonymic analogies. In this charm, each herb is called upon and reminded of its power.[11] One herb is to remember what it accomplished at "Regenmeld," another is reminded that

> over you the carts creaked, over you the queens rode,
> over you brides cried out, over you oxen snorted,

another once fought the snake, another is reminded of what it accomplished at "Alorford," and so on. These references are obscure, but it seems likely that they are drawn from pagan myth that is lost to us. In each case, the herb is said to have a particular power which it manifested at one time in the past. Thus, when the magician gathers and uses the herbs, she or he gathers and uses the particular powers metonymically attached to them. The lines referring to the nine herbs as a group are particularly interesting:

> These nine have power against nine poisons.
> A snake came crawling, he bit a man;
> then Woden took nine glory rods,
> struck the adder so that it flew into nine pieces.

Here Woden, known in Old High German and Old Norse texts as the *galdrsfaoir* 'the father of charms' (Storms 5), has successfully employed the nine herbs as a unit. This incident is an index of the power residing in the group of the herbs.[12]

"The Nine Herbs Charm" is rather more literary than the cattle charms and the pasture charm. The analogies are slightly more extended and thus more suggestive of brief narratives than the analogies of St. Helen, Herod, and so on found in the cattle charms. The vehicles chosen for the analogies in "Nine Herbs" seem likewise far removed in space and time from the tenor, which is probably a cure for snake bite, but they clearly show that the principle connecting the vehicle with the tenor is metonymic, for it employs representation rather than similarity. Each of these charms, "Swarm of Bees," "Unfruitful Land," the cattle charms, and "Nine Herbs" function by calling up certain powers and harnessing them to achieve the desired effect. The power to settle a swarm, to make a pasture productive, to find stolen cattle, or to cure a snake bite: these are powers not ordinarily in human possession—for the Anglo-Saxons at any rate. But these powers do exist: pasture can be fruitful, stolen things can be found, wounds can be cured. The trick is to obtain the power, and this is done metonymically, by seizing on an index of that power and bringing that index into the present to bear on the situation at hand.

Metaphoric Charms

The metaphoric charms are fewer than the metonymic, and most contain substantial metonymic sections. "Against a Wen" is a brief charm consisting entirely of a spell with no directions for action. It begins by personifying the wen:

> Wen, wen, little wen,
> you shall not build here, nor have any homestead,
> but you must go hence to the nearby hill,
> where you have an only brother, poor wretch.

Giving the wen human characteristics—it builds homesteads, can travel, has a brother, and can follow verbal commands—is a way of effecting the desired result. If the wen can be treated like a human being, then it can be told to depart. The concept of building is metaphoric: the growth of a tumor is similar to the gradual building of a house. The tenor (the wen) and the vehicle (a would-be homesteader who must be exiled) are very far distant from one another, as far distant as fire and orange light bulbs. There is no connection semantically or in space or time between a tumor and a human exile. The charm does conclude with metonymic analogies, but there is no calling up of powers beyond ordinary human control, nor is there any action for bringing the vehicles of these analogies into contact with the tenor:

> Shrink as coal on the hearth,
> shrivel as muck on the wall,
> and fade as water in a pitcher.
> Become as little as a grain of linseed,
> and much smaller than the hipbone of a handworm.
> become so small that you become naught.

Coal on a hearth, muck (?) on a wall, and water in a pitcher are all representatives of the set of things which gradually disappear. The similes instruct the wen to join this set. The linseed and the hipbone of a handworm are representatives of the set of things that are miniscule, and the similes again instruct the wen to join this set. The final injunction has the wen join the null set, and thus, disappear.

"A Journey Charm" likewise uses both metonymic analogies and a series of metaphors. Like "Against a Wen," it consists only of a verse spell with no directions. The charmer begins by stating that he protects himself with a staff and commends himself to God, both of which, God and the staff, will protect him from the dangers of travel. There follows a listing of biblical figures from which two half-lines of verse appear to have been dropped:

> May the Almighty, and the Son, and the Holy Spirit keep me well,
> the exalted Lord of all glory, as I heard the creator   of the heavens

* * * Abraham and Isaac
and such men, Moses and Jacob,
and David and Joseph, * * *
and Eve and Anne and Elizabeth,
Sarah and also Mary, Christ's mother,
and also the brothers Peter and Paul,
. . . .

The best sense one can make of this section is that the charmer is requesting the same protection that God gave to all these people. The well-known stories of these figures are indices for God's protective power, and the charmer desires to number himself among them.

The charm then continues:

May the hope of glory be for me
a hand over my head, a roof of saints,
a troop of victorious righteous angels.
I pray to all with a blithe mind
that Matthew be my helm, Mark my armor,
the bright covering of life, Luke my sword,
sharp and shining edged, John my shield,
made beautiful in glory, the seraphim my spear.

It ends with a request that the charmer may be *belucan*, literally 'locked up,' against the foe, "stationed" in the glory of angles and in the "holy hand." This section is one of the few spots in the metrical charms that employs metaphor to leap the boundary into the transcendent realm. Yet it does so by means of a metaphor that is very common in Anglo-Saxon literature: God as a Germanic chieftain. The vehicle and tenor of this metaphor are set up in the beginning of the charm: the traveler has a staff for physical protection and desires that the metaphysical protection afforded by God will act as the staff does. God is to place his hand metaphorically over the traveler's head, just as a thane's lord would do during pledging or gift-giving.[13] The depiction of the four evangelists and the seraphim as armor and weapons further suggests what Grendon calls the "Heathen notion of God's kingdom as a military power" (Grendon: 149). There are no similes here: the charmer simply asks that these things be. The metaphors require the reader's (and charmer's) denial of their literal truth. Sheer similarity operates alone here: the distance between tenors and vehicles is infinitely great.

"For Unfruitful Land B" makes similar use of transcendent metaphor in the midst of an otherwise metonymic charm. This charm for fields involves such metonymic action as placing seed in the plow, placing a loaf under the first furrow, and so on. But it also includes two prayers that are strikingly literary and metaphoric. Like the section of "A Journey Charm" discussed above, the controlling metaphor of these prayers leaps the boundary between the mundane and the transcendent and brings the action of the divine to bear in the worldly sphere. The first prayer begins:

> Erce, Erce, Erce, earth's mother
> May the All-powerful, the eternal Lord, grant you
> fields waxing and flourishing.
> bringing forth and strengthening
> shafts of millet, shining crops,
> and broad barley crops, and white wheat crops,
> and all the crops of the earth.
> . . . .

The second prayer in full reads:

> Be well, Earth, mother of men.
> Grow in God's embrace,
> filled with food for the use of men.

The identity of "Erce, Earth's mother" is unknown. *Erce* is clearly not an Old English name, and is probably Celtic in orgin.[14] In any event, Erce seems to be a primal goddess who is God's, or a god's, consort, and the offspring of their union are the crops. The word *eacniendra* 'bringing forth' is usually used of human pregnancy and *waestm*, 'fruit' or 'produce' often means 'fruit of the womb' or 'offspring.' In the second prayer, the word *faepm* 'embrace, bosom, or lap' suggests human sexual activity. Thus, like the extended metaphor in "A Journey Charm," these prayers imply a metaphysical world-view. In both charms, one Christian and the other pagan, human activity is metaphorically linked to divine activity.

Unlike the charms discussed thus far, which use both the metaphoric and the metonymic modes, "For a Sudden Stitch" is wholly and profoundly metaphoric. It begins with a brief herbal recipe, which includes feverfew, red nettle, and plantain, boiled in butter, and then plunges into its narrative:

Loud were they, lo, loud, when they rode over the barrow,
they were resolute when they rode over the land.
Shield yourself now, that you may survive this violence.
Out little spear, if you are within here.
I stood under the linden shield, under the light shield,
where the mighty women prepared their might
and sent yelling spears.
I will send one back to them,
a flying arrow in return.
Out little spear, if it is within here.
A smith sat, he struck a little knife
of iron, wondrously strange.
Out little spear if you are within here.
Six smiths sat, wrought slaughter-spears.
Out, spear, not in, spear.
If there is a piece of iron in here,
the work of a witch, heat will melt it.
. . . .
If it is a shot of the Esa, or a shot of the elves,
or a shot of the witches, I will help you.
. . . .

Then the charmer is instructed to put the knife, not previously mentioned, into the liquid, presumably the herb butter for which the recipe was given in the first lines.

The disease for which this charm is a remedy is *faerstice*: *faer* is a sudden attack by armed raiders and *stice* is a stab, sting, or prick. The disease is probably arthritis or lumbago, but the name *faerstice* is itself metaphoric, and sets up the metaphor for the entire charm. The homeopathic use of herbs continues the metaphor. Nettle stings, while plantain, as Howell D. Chickering, Jr. points out, has a spear-shaped head and feverfew has spear-shaped seeds. To boil these herbs in butter would soften them and thus deprive them of their power to harm (Chickering: 96–97). As vehicles for the pain, what happens to the herbs will happen to the pain as well. There is no stated analogy as in "Nine Herbs," no reference to past deeds which would serve as indices of the herbs' powers which the magician wishes to capture. The herbs' powers are wholly iconic: they stand for the pain because they are similar to it. This is not a striking metaphor; in fact, it is something of a dead metaphor, for it is commonplace to speak of a stabbing or shooting pain. In addition, there is evidence for widespread association of stabbing pain with supernatural beings, which is the basis of the narrative which follows the herbal recipe. For example, the German word for lumbago is *Hexenschuss*, and C. L. Wrenn points out that in northern England persons so afflicted are said to be "elfshotten" (Wrenn: 169). Arthritic pain feels like that inflicted with a knife, but the agent is invisible, and thus, in a magical context, supernatural. The agents of disease are the Esa (the Germanic gods) and witches, armed with iron weapons made by elves.[15] The pain itself is one of these weapons that has found its mark. The effect of this charm is not one of logic and inevitability. There is nothing as logical about recounting a battle over an arthritic victim as there is in, for example, casting earth over a swarm of bees. Instead, this charm makes a bold leap into a mythic realm where mundane pain is transformed into what L. M. C. Weston calls an "ur-battle" (Weston: 178).

In fine, the Old English metrical charms provide ample confirmation for the binary model of language. Contagious magic suggests metonymic progression of ideas and metonymic language, and results in logical, prosaic (although not necessarily prose) charms. Homeopathic magic, on the other hand, suggests metaphoric leaps of the imagination, rather than logical progression, and metaphoric language, and results in strikingly literary charms. But at the same time that these charms demonstrate the viability of the binary model of language, the model itself proves to be the key to the charms, just as it served as the key to modern novels for David Lodge. The binary model makes sense of the charms. Looked at through this theory, they are no longer quaint artifacts of unsophisticated minds, but living pieces of discourse that reflect not only the Anglo-Saxons' way of thinking, but our own as well.

NOTES

1. An edition and translation of selected charms by Felix Grendon appeared in 1909, the entire corpus was edited and translated by Gotfrid Storms in 1948, and the *Lacnunga* was edited and translated by Grattan and Singer in 1952. The twelve Old English metrical charms appeared in 1942 in the sixth volume of Krapp and Dobbie's *Anglo-Saxon Poetic Records*, whose edition and titles will be used here.

2. "An incoherent jumbling of words, miscellaneously derived from Latin, Greek, Hebrew, Gaelic, and other languages" (Grendon: 114).

3. Webster grants the spell and the act equal standing (Webster: 92) and believes that the spell alone is efficacious (Webster: 69), while Evans-Pritchard states that "[t]here is no power in the address itself" (Evans-Pritchard: 450). Leach believes that magical performances "invariably" include a spell (Leach: 30), while Storms believes that spells are added to acts only when magic is in decline in a society (Storms: 144). Nöth, writing specifically on the Old English charms, likewise believes the spell to be optional.

4. Nelson investigates speech acts in three of the metrical charms.

5. Storms questions the purpose of these narrative sections (Storms: 33), as does Bacon, who points out that this question is closely related to that of whether the power of the charm resides in the spell or in the act. Wicker sees the narrative as essential to magic. Because magical occurrence, by its very nature, cannot be observed, the magician resorts to a story as "the only way in which this kind of connection between cause and effect... can be displayed" (Wicker: 43-44).

6. The distinction between prayer and spell is maintained by Storms: 47–48, 178, 221; Bowra: 117, 278); Webster: 111–112; Weston: 177; and others, in addition to Frazer and Jakobson. Evans-Pritchard distinguishes between the prayer as an address made to a spiritual being and the spell as an address made to an object in which mystical power resides (Evans-Pritchard: 10). Murray and Rosalie Wax: 495–500 provide a good summary of the controversy and suggest that the dichotomy is invalid. Butler: ix and Webster: 111–112 both maintain that the two modes are often inseparable.

7. For explicit references to Saussure and Jakobson, see *The Savage Mind* (149–150 and note).

8. The *ASPR* cites A. R. Skemp's division at line 38 (cxxxiii), although lines 39–44 clearly continue the first charm. Storms

recognizes two parts (Storms: 172–178), while Rosenberg and Nelson treat the charm as a unit.

9. Rosenberg: 431 and Storms: 8, 182, and passim, for example, understand the crosses to be sun symbols here.

10. Thus Rosenberg: 435, Storms: 180, and Grendon: 155.

11. Old English plant names are notoriously slippery, and this charm contains several hapax legomena as well. For various attempts to identify each herb, see the *ASPR* notes, Merony, and Vaughn-Sterling.

12. I follow Abernathy: 68 and Storms: 191 here, who both argue convincingly that Woden's nine sticks are the nine herbs. Storms's theory that these lines have been misplaced by the scribe is persuasive.

13. There are numerous examples of this metaphor in the literature: Tupper points out evidence in "The Wanderer" (lines 41–44) and of the term *mundbora* 'handshield' which is frequently used of God. See also Amies, especially p. 451.

14. Thus Druckert. Boenig provides a summary of the various interpretaions of *erce* (Boenig: 130, note 1).

15. For attempts to identify the characters of the narrative with the Esa, elves, and witches, see Hauer, Doskow, and Skemp: 292.

REFERENCES

Abernathy, George William. 1983. "The Germanic Metrical Charms." Diss. University of Wisconsin.

Amies, Marion. 1983. "The Journey Charm: A Lorica for Life's Journey." *Neophilologus* 67: 448–462.

Austin, John. 1961. *Philosophical Papers*. Ed. J. O. Urmson and G. J. Warnock. Oxford: Oxford University Press.

Bacon, I. 1952. "Versuch einer Klassifizierung altdeutscher Zaubersprüche und Segen." *MLN* 67: 224–232.

Barley, Nigel. 1972. "Anglo-Saxon Magico-Medicine." *Journal of the Anthropological Society of Oxford* 3: 67–77.

Boenig, Robert. 1983. "*Erce* and Dew." *Names* 31: 130–131.

Bowra, C. M. 1962. *Primitive Song*. Cleveland: World Publishing.

Browne, Roger M. 1971. "The Typology of Literary Signs." *CE* 33: 1–17.

Butler, Eliza M. 1949. *Ritual Magic*. Cambridge: Cambridge University Press.

Chickering, Howell D., Jr. 1971. "The Literary Magic of *Wið Færstice*." *Viator* 2: 83–104.

Doskow, Minna. 1976. "Poetic Structure and the Problem of Smiths in 'Wið Færstice.' "*PLL* 12: 321–326.

Duckert, Audrey R. 1972. "*Erce* and Other Possibly Keltic Elements in the Old English Charm for Unfruitful Land." *Names* 20: 83–90.

Evans-Pritchard, E. E. 1937. *Witchcraft, Oracle and Magic among the Azande* . London: Oxford University Press.

Frazer, Sir James G. 1922. *The Golden Bough*. Abridged ed. New York: Macmillan.

Grattan, J. H. G. and Charles Singer. 1952. *Anglo-Saxon Magic and Medicine.* London: Oxford University Press.

Grendon, Felix. 1909. "The Anglo-Saxon Charms." *JAF* 22: 105–235.

Hauer, Stanley R. 1978. "Structure and Unity in the Old English Charm *Wið Færstice*." *ELN* 15: 250–257.

Hill, Thomas D. 1978. "The Theme of the Cosmological Cross in Two Old English Cattle Theft Charms." *N&Q* 25: 488–490.

Jakobson, Roman. (a) 1960. "Closing Statement: Linguistics and Poetics." In *Style in Language* . Ed. Thomas A. Sebeok. Cambridge, MA: MIT: 350–377.

———. (b) 1956. "Two Aspects of Language and Two Types of Asphasic Disturbances." In *Fundamentals of Language*. Jakobson and Morris Halle. New York: Mouton: 67–96.

Krapp, G. P. and E. V. K. Dobbie. 1931–1932. *The Anglo-Saxon Poetic Records*. New York: Columbia University Press.

Leach, Edmund. 1976. *Culture and Communication*. Cambridge: Cambridge University Press.

Levi-Strauss, Claude. 1966. *The Savage Mind*. Chicago: University of Chicago Press, 1966.

Lodge, David. 1977. *The Modes of Modern Writing*. Ithaca, NY: Cornell University Press.

Nelson, Marie. 1984. "'Wordsige and Worcsige': Speech Acts in Three Old English Charms." *Language and Style* 17: 57–66.

Magoun, Francis P. 1943. "OE Charm A13: *butan heardan beaman*." *MLN* 58: 33–34.

Meroney, Howard. 1944. "The Nine Herbs." *MLN* 59: 157–160.

Nöth, Winfried. 1977. "Semiotics of the Old English Charms." *Semiotica* 19: 59–83.

Peirce, Charles Sanders. 1955. *Philosophical Writings of Peirce*. Ed. Justus Buchler. New York: Dover.

Rosenberg, Bruce. 1966. "The Meaning of Æcerbot." *JAF* 79: 428–436.

Saussure, Ferdinand de. 1966. *Course in General Linguistics*. New York: McGraw-Hill.

See, Fred G. 1974. "The Demystification of Style: Metaphoric and Metonymic Language in *A Modern Instance*." *Nineteenth Century Fiction* 28: 379–403.

Skemp, A. R. 1911. "The Old English Charms." *MLR* 6: 289–301.

Storms, Godfrid. 1948. *Anglo-Saxon Magic*. The Hague: Nijhoff.

Tupper, F., Jr. 1912. "Notes on Old English Poems, v: Hand ofer Heafod." *JEGP* 11: 97–100.

Vaughan-Sterling, Judith A. 1983. "The Anglo-Saxon *Metrical Charms*: Poetry as Ritual." *JEGP* 82: 186–200.

Wax, Murray and Rosalie. 1963. "The Notion of Magic." *Current Anthropology* 4: 495–518.

Webster, Hutton. 1948. *Magic: A Sociological Study*. Stanford, CA: Stanford University Press.

Weston, L. M. C. 1985. "The Language of Magic in Two Old English Metrical Charms." *NM* 86: 176–186.

Wicker, Brian. 1975. *The Story-Shaped World*. Notre Dame, IN: University of Notre Dame Press.

Wrenn, C. L. 1967. *A Study of Old English Literature*. New York: Norton.

CHAPTER SEVEN

THE LESSON OF THE BESTIARY

Gary Shank

The medieval bestiary is a total mystery to the modern mind. We see this quaint form as a relic of a darker age, a throwback to an era of ignorance and contempt for the sort of careful observing and theorizing that has built the modern world. And yet, the bestiary refuses to die. Scholarly research on the bestiary has persisted, with several important studies in this century alone (Carmody, Cook, Cronin, Ladner, and Thorndike, just to name a few). In the past half century or so, we have seen a new edition of a twelfth-century Latin bestiary (White), a facsimile of a 15th century Latin bestiary (Davis), a new version of the medieval classic *The Phoenix* (Blake), a new translation of *Physiologus* (Curley), a new rendering of a late medieval lyrical bestiary (Elliot), and new editions of such classics as *The Bestiary of Love* (de Fournival, ca. 1246–1260 A.D.), and *The Garden of Eloquence* (Peachem, see Espy). In addition, there has been a spate of brand new bestiaries written for the modern reader. Some, like *An Odd Bestiary* (Block and Robinson) attempt to re-construct the medieval bestiary. Others attempt to push the bestiary form into new arenas of consideration. For example, Borges has written *The Book of Imaginary Being*, Willard Espy offers *A Rhetorical Bestiary*, Gillespie and Mechling describe American animals, and even George Plimpton has written a curiosity which he calls *A Sports Bestiary*. Roger Knutson's *Flattened Fauna*, which is a guidebook for identifying the shapes and natures of road-smashed creatures, is possibly the strangest addition to the lot.

Why does the bestiary carry such fascination to the modern mind? How has it changed as a form over the years? What lesson does it deliver about the textual nature of animals, and nature of texts themselves? These questions require new insights and new methods of inquiry. For the past several years I have been working on a semiotic method of inquiry which I call "juxtapositional analysis". The fundamental assumption of justapositional analysis is that any two objects of inquiry can be juxtaposed, thereby leading the inquirer to draw meaningful conclusions about the said juxtaposition. In particular, one way to advance the understanding of the juxtaposition is to describe the first component by using the language of the second component. By shifting both the language and the context of the first component, new insights about that component should be uncovered.

The purpose of this paper is to do such an analysis, so as to shed new light on the nature and history of the bestiary, and its place in the modern world. The idea of the bestiary, then, is the "text" of this particular semiotic methodology. In this way, we should be able to trace the textual thread of the bestiary from the medieval world to see its modern counterpart (see van den Broek, in press, for a semiotic analysis of medieval herbaria).

The first premise of juxtapositional analysis is to choose the items of the juxtaposition carefully, so as to advance the project. In this case, one of my terms was pre-determined; namely, the idea and nature of the bestiary. To get the other term, I had to consider the aim of my research endeavor. I decided to use the notion (from the computer world) of the Expert Systems Database (hereafter abbreviated as ESD) as the second component of the justaposition. Even though my knowledge of ESDs was confined to what I have read in the popular press and in computer magazines, nonetheless I felt that even my rudimentary knowledge of the concept would be enough to initiate a meaningful analysis. Scholars in the computer world are certainly free to provide their insights and thereby to extend this inquiry, once it has been started.

There are several compelling reason to use the ESD as the second component of the juxtapositional anaylsis. First of all, an ESD is essentially a computerized system of information organized in a way so as to allow for flexible access, and which also comes with a set of inference rules to help make "expert" judgments about classifying and responding to various cases of information. As such, it is clearly a modern notion, and thereby intelligible to modern inquiry (and inquirers). Secondly, ESDs seem to share several key properties with bestiaries, including the ability to organize information from a variety of sources. Thirdly, ESDs should give us enough flexibility to treat bestiaries in their various transformations at different times in history, since they themselves have undergone various generations of change in recent history. Finally, the ESD seems to be an example of a truly emerging form of textuality. That is, the modern concepts of technology are "textual" in the sense that we have evolved past the idea of looking at the natural world as a "book" that can be read by scientists (cf. Josipovici). Now, we tend to look at the world as a vast "database", where all we need are the appropriate algorithms and heuristic strategies to convert the information from the database into valuable applied knowledge. Therefore, the very idea of textuality in our times requires the consideration of ideas such as the database and the operation of information systems in general.

In order to begin our analysis, we need to lay out the parameters for our comparison. In this case, our defining parameters will come from the ESD side, and they will be applied to what we know about bestiaries. ESDs have a variety of components that are crucial for this juxtaposition. Every ESD needs a data operating system, or DOS, to serve as its basic program source. That is, the SOS is the framework for programming and access of ESDs. Also, an ESD needs a source database. The source database is simply the place where the ESD gets its basic information, or "raw data." Judgment rules about cases and classifications are handled by discriminatory algorithms and heuristic rules. Finally, all ESDs need an interpreter, or language of operation. The interpreter allows the user to go back and forth between the DOS and the ESD. Now, let us apply these ESD principles to bestiaries, and see what happens.

* * * * *

In the ancient world, there were many chronicles of the natures, histories, and habits of animals. These data were compiled by such famous programmers as Aristotle (ca. 340 B.C.), Aelian (ca. 200 A.D.), and Pliny (late 1st Century A.D.). Each programmer had his own strengths and weaknesses. Aristotle, for instance, was the prime authority on animals in the ancient world, but his interests were focused on the study and explanation of general principles and properties, rather than on the nature of specific animals as such (cf. Balme; Gotthelf). Pliny described various animals in detail, but his work was not very systematic. Aelian described even more animals, with great literary skill, but was even more disorganized than Pliny.

General problems persisted across all of these classical programs. Cross-referencing and gaining access to particular facets of the data were cumbersome projects at best. This state of affairs persisted until sometime between the second and the fourth centuries A.D. At this time, we have the first true ESD regarding animals. No one knows who the clever programmer was who instituted this system, but we do know that he worked out of Alexandria. His program was a crude model in many ways, barely more than a prototype. Called the *Physiologus*, it consisted of only 49 entries (Curley). There was no capacity for graphics, not even crude black-and-white drawings. There was no apparent system of hierarchical order. Lions were put next to lambs, so to speak. Finally, the programmer of *Physiologus* apparently had a poor discriminatory algorithm, since he included trees and rocks as part of the database.

It is hard for us, from our lofty perspective, to appreciate the breakthrough that *Physiologus* achieved. Simply put, this compendium was the first document to create a common base of referrence for animal stories, thereby pulling all of these entries together as a genuine cohesive text. In this case, the DOS was the Bible. Using the Bible as a basis for allegorical interpretation was an idea that flourished in Alexandria in the 2nd century A.D., and which was given its mature form by Augustine (ca. 396–427). Augustine supported the idea that many of the tales of the Bible were best understood as allegories, an idea which Origen of Alexandria (ca. 2nd century A.D.) and others had refined and extended to include the entire world and all its creatures. Crude though it was, *Physiologus* managed to use its interpreter (in this case, Greek) to interface Christian teaching and animal lore. Once Augustine finalized the allegorical project as an integral part of Christian understanding, we find the unfolding of an age, lasting for a thousand years in the medieval west, where the bestiary is a prime example of the process of understanding the relationship between the word of God and the nature of the world. In the work that we call the *Physiologus*, all of the moral, analogical, and anagogical meanings of the animal stories gleaned from the programmers mentioned earlier were tied together within this remarkable ESD.

Like any good technological innovation, the bestiary was subject to change. Over the centuries, we find a refinement of this first generation ESD. The second generation represents several major modifications, and many enhancements of the original model. Here, we are considering the Latin Bestiary of the Twelfth Century, primarily as found in England (White). The DOS remains the Bible. The database has been greatly expanded and organized, with much of the organization written in Isidore, a hierarchical encyclopedic treatment of the material described by earlier animal programmers (McCullough: 28). Isidore allows us to organize animals in terms of various categories, and is powerful enough to eliminate borderline cases like fig trees and Piroboli rocks. With the organization afforded by Isidore, we find a great expansion of data, with up to 250 entries. The interpreter has shifted from Greek to Latin, and the function of the ESD has been upgraded so as to expand, organize, and codify animal lore, especially as rendered through Isidore, while sustaining, wherever possible, the Christian teachings that were the focus of the first generation. Notice, however, for the first time, the presence of database entries without specific Christian moral references. Another important upgrade was the addition of a powerful graphics mode. This mode took the form of line drawings of animals, color paintings, and a particularly intriguing special feature called Illuminated Manuscripts, which was especially useful in highlighting the first letter of the first word of the entries.

Technology never stands still, and this is the case with the bestiaries as well. By the end of the Twelfth century and the beginning of the Thirteenth, we have a third generation of bestiaries. This variant in many ways is more modest than its immediate predecessor, but it nonetheless incorporates several key improvements. We can call this example the Metrical Bestiary (e.g. Theobold, ca. 11th century/1928). The Metrical Bestiary is generally much smaller than its ancestors, in most cases with a capacity of only 12 to 15 entries. Isidore is still the source database, but it is a truncated version of Isidore, which we might call mini-Isidore. As was the case for the two earlier generations, the Bible is still the DOS. The great change that was instituted was the presence of an artistic function for its own sake, as shown by the fact that the entries were all written in rhymed Latin. Some might argue that the Metrical Bestiary was designed as a teaching device, thus explaining its small size and its use of easy-to-remember rhymes. Whether or not it represents a separate generation of bestiaries, therefore, remains controversial.

There is no question that the next generation of bestiaries represents a crucial change. Here, in the fourth generation, we find the last contribution of the medieval period to the bestiary form. In fact, we can call this generation the Proto-Modern Bestiary. With the proto-modern bestiary, we have the greatest technological shift in the field since the inception of the bestiary itself. All prior generations, from *Physiologus* to the Latin and metrical Bestiaries, shared the common assumption that the primary role of the bestiary was to bring about a link between natural observation and Christian teachings. Since Christian teachings, like all religious teachings, are essentially rhetorical in form, there existed the possibility of shifting the rhetorical base of the bestiary away from Christianity, towards some other position. This shift constitutes the fourth generation of bestiaries. The most famous example of the proto-modern Bestiary was Richard de Fournival's *Bestiary of Love* (ca. 1246–1260) and the subsequent response by an unknown woman. Here we have the standard bestiary fare modified in order to create an appeal for seduction.

With the appearance of the Proto-Modern Bestiary, we have evidence for decline of the bestiary as a general form. The stories and legends that serve as the basis for the observational content of bestiaries come under increasing attack by the emerging disciplines of modern science, and biology in particular. In 1643, Sir Thomas Browne published *Vulgar Errors*, which is essentially a refutation of many of these stories, and so serves as the first true anti-bestiary (in Browne). This anti-bestiary sentiment led to the formation of zoological treatises that are the beginning of our modern scientific understanding of animal data (e.g. Topsell; Ley).

By the modern era, we have the arrival of the fifth, and so far, final, generation of bestiaries. The modern bestiary has drawn away from earlier accounts of animals, with the exception of a handful of animals that are known definitely *not* to exist. These accounts can be scholarly (e.g. Rowland, South, and Shepard) or popular (e.g. Silverberg). So, the fairy-tale form becomes the DOS for the modern bestiary. The database consists of fanciful and amusing erroneous and imaginary accounts from the past about such fauna as unicorns, griffins, dragons, and so on. The modern bestiary must be beautiful in form, and many of them are illustrated profusely (e.g. Block and Elliot). Very often, special typefaces and facsimile calligraphy scripts are used to highlight the "one-of-a-kind" look of these books.

* * * * *

If we trace the evolution of the DOSs used in the various generations of bestiaries, then we reach a clear and interesting conclusion. The initial DOS, the one that organized the first three generations, emphasized the rhetorical power of the Bible as a device to understand the lives and habits of animals as texts. Here, we have the well-known notion that, in the middle ages, the world was seen as the book of God, meant to be read for its moral lessons. The bestiary was a reading aid for understanding that part of the book of God that was about animals. When the idea of the book of God disintegrated, it appeared that the bestiary was doomed. Rather than fade away, though, it became transformed. The rhetorical power was shifted away from the Bible, and put in the hands of any skillful person pressing an argument. So long as these stories had power, they were used to persuade. The rise of science spelled the end of the persuasive power of these ancient animal tales. Yet, again, the bestiary refused to die. Instead, it drew its power from those stories that were precisely shown to be always in error, those accounts that could never be true. The DOS of the modern bestiary became a rhetoric of the private, the unverifiable, the perpetually hidden and undiscoverable, coded in the guise of the fabulous and the imaginary.

This rhetorical shift can be captured by the notions of the database and the text. The earliest writers who documented the natural histories of animals were attempting to deal with facts, and to describe actual animals. If there were griffins and unicorns and manticores in their accounts, these creatures were present because the chroniclers felt that they did indeed exist. The plausibility of these creatures was determined by the plausibility of narrative accounts of travellers to the far-off lands where these animals were presumed to dwell. Eyewitness accounts and stories in general are no longer considered to be valid sources of information. Information is anything that can be symbolically rendered, and the result of any valid computation on such rendered data. The power of computation has replaced the power of meaning, and so the database has come to replace the text. Therefore, the bestiary can amuse us, because it is about story, but it cannot inform us, since it is not about data that can

148

be separated from story and manipulated on its own terms. Is this the end of the bestiary? We now live in an era where faantastic computational power, as manifested in computer databases, allow us access to vast amounts of information in mere seconds. We know more about animals today than we have ever known. There seems to be no room for conjecture, and so the bestiary seems destined to survive as an archaic form of entertainment.

What would happen, though, if we consciously adopted a semiotic DOS for the database, to create the post-modern, or semiotic, bestiary. We do know more now than ever before about animals, but we know next to nothing about what animals mean. Our systems of knowledge, as exemplified by ESDs, have become computational, and thereby divorced from the ancient tradition of putting knowledge in a narrative form. With a semiotic bestiary, we could look upon our knowledge as a set of clues about the nature of reality, waiting to be organized into stories about how animals can tell us about our world. The sixth generation, if it ever comes, would be the most radical yet. For the first time, the form would be freed from its dependence on rhetorical persuasion as its DOS. A semiotic DOS would let the clues of the world talk for themselves, and the bestiary would finally become the sophisticated instrument of inquiry that it is capable of being.

REFERENCES

Ælian. ca. 200 A.D./1658. *On Animals*. In 3 volumes. A. F. Scholfield, trans. Cambridge, MA: Harvard University Press.

Aristotle. ca. 340 B.C./1984. "History of animals." In *The Complete Works of Aristotle, Volume 1*. J. Barnes, trans. Princeton, NJ: Princeton University Press.

Augustine, St. ca. 396–427 A.C./1958. *On Christian Doctrine*. D. W. Robertson, Jr., trans. Indianapolis, IN: Bobbs-Merrill Educational Publishing.

Balme, D. B. 1975. "Aristotle's use of diffenentiæ in zoology." In *Articles on Aristotle: 1. Science* . J. Barnes, M. Schofield, and R. Sorabji, eds. London: Duckworth.

Blake, N. F., ed. ca. 1072/1964. *The Phoenix*. Manchester: Manchester University Press.

Borges, J. L. with Guerrero, M. 1967/1969. *The Book of Imaginary Beings* . N.T. di Giovanni, trans.. NY: Avon Books.

van den Broek, G. J. In press. "Botany as semiosis." For *Semiotica Mediævalia,* a special issue of *Semiotica* , J. Evans, ed.

Browne, Sir Thomas. 1643/1862. *Religio Medici and Other Papers* . Boston, MA: Ticknor and Fields.

Carmody, F. J. 1938. *"De Bestiis and Aliis Rebus* and the Latin Physiologue." *Speculum* 13: 153–159.

Cook, A. S., trans. late 8th Century A.D./1921. *The Old English Physiologus*. New Haven, CT: Yale University Press.

Cronin, G., Jr. 1941. "The Bestiary and the Mediæval Mind— Some Complexities." *Modern Language Quarterly* 2: 191– 198.

Curley, M. J., trans. ca. 2nd to 5th Centuries/1979. *Physiologus*. Austin, TX: University of Texas Press.

Davis, J. I., comp. and intro. 15th Century/1958. *Libellus de Natura Animalum* . London: Dawson's of Pall Mall.

Elliot, T. J., trans. and intro. ca. 13th Century/1971. *A Medieval Bestiary* . Boston, MA: Godine.

Espy, W. R. 1986. *The Garden of Eloquence: A Rhetorical Bestiary* (including portions of the first *Garden of Eloquence* published in 1577 by H. Peachem). NY: Harper and Row.

de Fournival, R. ca. 1246-1260/1986. *Master Richard's Bestiary of Love and Response*. J. Beer, trans. Berkeley, CA: University of California Press.

Gillespie, A. K. and Mechling, J., eds. 1987. *American Wildlife in Symbol and Story*. Knoxville, TN: University of Tennessee Press.

Gottheif, A. 1988. "Historiæ I: plaantarum et animalium." In *Theophrastean Studies, Volume III* . W. W. Fortenbaugh and R. W. Sharples, eds. New Brunswick, NJ: Transaction Books.

Josipovici, G. 1971. *The World and the Book*. Stanford, CA: Stanford University Press.

Knutson, R. M. 1987. *Flattened Fauna*. Berkeley, CA: Ten Speed Press.

Ladner, G. B. 1979. "Medieval and Modern Understanding of Symbolism: A Comparison." *Speculum* 44: 223–256.

Ley, W. 1968. *Dawn of Zoology* . Englewood Cliffs, NJ: Prentice-Hall, Inc.

McCullough, F. 1960. *Mediæval Latin and French Bestiaries*. Chapel H ill, NC: The University of North Carolina Press.

Origen. ca. 2nd Century A.D./1982. "Homilies on Genesis and Exodus." R. E. Heine, trans. In *The Fathers of the Church Series*. Washington, DC: The Catholic University of America Press.

Plimpton, G. 1982. *A Sports Bestiary* . NY: McGraw-Hill.

Pliny. late First Century A.D./1946. *Natural History: Books Eight to Eleven*. Volume Three of the English Translation, H. Rackham, trans. Cambridge, MA: Harvard University Press.

Rowland, B. 1973. *Animals with Human Faces: A Guide to Animal Symbolism*. Knoxville, TN: University of Tennessee Press.

Shepard, O. 1930/1982. *The Lore of the Unicorn*. NY: Metropolitan Museum of Art.

Silverberg, B., ed. o. 1973. *Phoenix Feathers* . NY: E. P.Dutton and Co.

South, M., ed. 1987. *Mythical and Fabulous Creatures*. NY: Greenwood Press.

Theobald, Bishop. ca. 11th Century/1928. *Physiologus: A Metrical Bestiary of Twelve Chapters*. A.W. Rendell, trans. London: John and Edward Bumpus, LTD.

Thorndike, L. 1923. *A History of Magic and Experimental Science During the First Thirteen Centuries of Our Era*. Volume 1. NY: Columbia University Press.

Topsell, E. 1658/facsimile edition 1967. *The History of Four-Footed Beasts and Serpents and Insects, Taken Principally from the "Historiæ Animalium" of Conrad Gesner*. NY: Da Capo Press.

White, T.H. Trans. and Ed. 1954/1984. *The Book of Beasts: Being a Translation from a Latin Bestiary of the Twelfth Century*. NY: Dover Publications.

CONTRIBUTORS

Jonathan Evans is Associate Professor of English at the University of Georgia, Athens.

Karin Boglund-Lagopoulos is Faculty of the School of English at the University of Thessaloniki, Greece.

Mikle D. Ledgerwood is Assistant Professor of French and associated Professor in four other departments at the University at Stony Brook, New York.

SunHee Kim Gertz is Associate Professor of English at Clark University.

Lois Bragg is Associate Professor of English at Galludet College in Washington, D.C.

Mavis G. Fionella is Associate Professor of English at Fordham University, Lincoln Center, New York, New York.

Gary Shank is Associate Professor of Psychology at Northern Illinois University.

Studies on Themes and Motifs in Literature

The series is designed to advance the publication of research pertaining to themes and motifs in literature. The studies cover cross-cultural patterns as well as the entire range of national literature's. They trace the development and use of themes and motifs over extended periods, elucidate the significance of specific themes or motifs for the formation of period styles, and analyze the unique structural function of themes and motifs. By examining themes or motifs in the work of an author or period, the studies point to the impulses authors received from literary tradition, the choices made, and the creative transformation of the cultural heritage. The series will include publications of colloquia and theoretical studies that contribute to a greater understanding of literature.

For additional information about this series or for the submission of manuscripts, please contact:

Peter Lang Publishing
Acquisitions Dept.
516 N. Charles St., 2nd Floor
Baltimore, MD 21201